AF522434

20 GREATEST ENTREPRENEURS OF THE WORLD

RAMESH KUMAR

PRABHAT PRAKASHAN

No part of this publication can be reproduced, stored in a retrieval system or transmitted in any form or by any means, electronic, mechanical, photocopying, recording or otherwise, without prior permission of the author. Rights of this book are with the author.

Published by
PRABHAT PRAKASHAN PVT. LTD.
4/19 Asaf Ali Road,
New Delhi-110 002 (INDIA)
e-mail: prabhatbooks@gmail.com

ISBN 978-93-5521-789-9
20 GREATEST ENTREPRENEURS OF THE WORLD
by Ramesh Kumar

© Reserved

Edition
First, 2023

Price
₹ 250 (Rupees Two Hundred Fifty Only)

Printed at
Sanjay Printers, Sahibabad

Author's Note

From time to time, we all look for inspiration around us. And no one inspires us more than someone who had a humble beginning but grew to become a great success. Someone who possesses the courage to take on risks to start and run a business venture to create and deliver innovative products, services or solutions that meet a need in the marketplace. Throughout history, there have been many successful entrepreneurs, each with their own unique approach and contributions to the world of business. Every entrepreneur has a distinctive outlook but one thing common in all of them is their drive to achieve their goals.

To become a successful entrepreneur, one requires a combination of skills, including creativity, innovation, leadership, risk-taking, and a willingness to learn from failures. Successful entrepreneurs possess a deep understanding of their industry and the needs of their customers, as well as the ability to identify and pursue opportunities for growth.

There is no single specific list of the greatest or most extraordinary entrepreneurs, as several outstanding and talented people have made their contributions to our economic society. In this book, we will discuss the twenty greatest entrepreneurs of all time. They all had made a mark in their concerned industries with their zealous efforts and unwavering faith in their vision of a better world. From Jeff Bezos to Walt Disney, from Elon Musk to Mukesh Ambani and from Henry Ford to JRD Tata, all have been mentioned in this book.

With the means of this book, the author has made an attempt to share the story of some exceptional entrepreneurs who are an inspiration to all. Hopefully, this book will serve as a motivation and help the readers to learn some indispensable lessons on how to become a successful businessperson.

❑

Contents

1.
Jeff Bezos

The river Amazon is nearly 6400 kilometres long and is the largest river in the world by volume. In length, the Amazon is the second longest river in world.

The word Amazon signifies massive, formidable presence, very much like the company created by Jeff Bezos, its founder.

Bezos is an American entrepreneur, and the founder & CEO of Amazon. As on April 2021, he had a net worth of more than $200 billion USD and is one of the wealthiest persons in the world. In 2021, he decided to transition to a new role by 2021 as the Executive Chairman of the Amazon Board.

By then, Amazon would have further cemented its position as the most innovative and influential company in the world, with a revenue of nearly 386.064 billion in 2020.

Its iconic founder is notoriously private.

Bezos founded Amazon in 1994, commencing the journey of the company as an online bookstore, eventually expanding the company's services into a wide variety of e-commerce merchandise and eventually expanding the company's footprint to digital media such as video and audio streaming, cloud computing and artificial intelligence.

Three years after Bezos founded Amazon, he took it public with an Initial Public Offering (IPO). In 2003, Amazon rebounded from financial instability and turned a profit of $400 million.

Amazon has been accomplishing one milestone after another since its inception, right from the launch of Amazon Prime Video, Amazon Music, Audible, Twitch, Amazon Publishing, Amazon Studios, Amazon Web Services, apart from Kindle, Fire tablets, Fire TV, and Echo devices. In 2018, Amazon Prime acquired 100 million subscribers worldwide.

Bezos also founded Blue Origin in 2000, a company that manufactures aerospace materials and operates sub-orbital spaceflight services. Blue Origin achieved a milestone in 2015 when its New Shepard vehicle accomplished a successful space flight and returned to earth. It is also working on launching the commercial suborbital human spaceflight. In 2013, Bezos purchased *The Washington Post* for $250 million, expanding his business further into digital media.

Amazon has received its fair share of criticism over the years, and has been accused of anti-competitive behaviour, technological surveillance overreach, and tax avoidance.

Bezos's net worth has been continuously increasing and hit $150 billion in July 2018. He was recognised as the first centibillionaire on the *Forbes* wealth index and named the richest man in modern history. In August 2020, his net worth further increased to $200 billion, growing by approximately $24 billion during the time of the pandemic.

Early Years

Bezos was born in Albuquerque, was academically bright, and was a valedictorian in high school, and a National Merit Scholar, eventually making his way to Princeton University, for a degree in electrical engineering and computer science, graduating in 1986.

He started his career by working at a fintech telecom start-up, called Fitel. At Fitel, he was responsible for building a network for international trade. Soon after, he was promoted to head of development and director of customer service. After Fitel, Bezos pivoted and worked in the banking industry, joining the Bankers Trust as a product manager, from 1988 to 1990. After that stint, Bezos joined D. E. Shaw & Co, a hedge fund with a focus on mathematical modelling, from 1990 to 1994.

Bezos had already decided to work in the area of an internet enabled business, and decided to proceed with building an online bookstore. Leaving his job in 1994, he founded Amazon from his garage in the same year, with an initial investment of $300,000 from his parents.

Management Lessons Learnt from Jeff Bezos

Relentless Innovation

At Amazon, innovation has been one of the fundamental drivers of growth. The desire to experiment has been an integral part of Amazon's culture. Amazon has led several innovations right from simple ones such as customer reviews to one-click shopping, personalized recommendations, to huge disruptive innovations such as Just Walk Out shopping, Alexa.

Bezos obsession with constant innovation can be evidenced by the sheer scope of Amazon, right from Amazon Go stores, Prime Air (enabling customers to get their orders delivered in 30 minutes or less via drones who drop them at your doorstep) to Alexa, Amazon Web Services, Amazon is one company in which innovation is everyday life.

Company Culture

Bezos is said to have instilled a strong Day 1 mentality in Amazon, till date. Even though Amazon is nearly 25 years old, the company and its employees treats every day like it's the first day of their journey.

"Day 2 is stasis. Followed by irrelevance. Followed by excruciating, painful decline. Followed by death. And that is why it is always Day 1." –**Jeff Bezos**.

Bezos believes that staying hungry and relevant is incredibly important – and that comes if you treat every day like your first. Hence, Day 1.

A Day 2 mentality happens when a company expands, adjusts, decision making becomes slow, and becomes less agile, focuses more on internal challenges rather than customer and innovation.

The Day 1 mentality focuses the company to remain agile and nimble footed and quick to respond.

Decision making

Bezos is said to have urged employees to bet on ideas that have unlimited upside. He has repeatedly been cited in the media that he doesn't deliberate over easily reversible decisions. Quick decision making is a hallmark of a fast growing company.

This "bias for action" has been widely adopted by nearly all employees as it is cited as one of Amazon's 14 leadership principles. Speed matters in business and more so at Amazon. The company values calculated risk-taking.

It has been seen that most decisions can be made with around 70% of the information at hand. Access to more information can cost us time and does not radically improve decision making, as any challenges can be corrected by course correcting.

Quick decision making frees up executive bandwidth and allows the company to be more nimble and agile.

Thinking about the Customer

Amazon's mission statement is "to be the earth's most customer-centric company". This is also emblemed in their Leadership Principles, and has been at the front and centre of every decision in the company.

Bezos has attributed Amazon's success to being obsessed with customer experience. Right from the early days, he used to place an empty chair in the meetings to help executives think from the customer's perspective.

When Bezos was considering expanding Amazon beyond books and music, he conducted a survey amongst a group of customers enquiring what would they like to buy on the site. This supported his decision to expand Amazon to a wide array of merchandise.

Start with the customer and work backwards.

This motto allows Amazon to be more customer focused and pioneering. Much of Amazon's profit is directed back towards development projects that further enhance the customer experience.

Amazon has been constantly building leverage with innovative technologies [such as machine learning] to deliver on the customer promise. They also weave data with business goals and make mined data structured, clear and actionable for other departments so that every department can process and act on it, identifying high-value customer segments for their business strategies. The superior customer experience at Amazon is a result of the datafication of every customer exchange. Right from Amazon's frictionless customer journeys (1-click check out, low prices, 2-day shipping, Alexa reminders), product recommendations, reviews, everything in Amazon is customer-based and customer-first.

Long-Term Perspective

In his first letter to Amazon's shareholders, Bezos had stated that Amazon would always take the long-term perspective. He was clear, then and now, that Amazon would never choose decisions in favour of optimizing quarterly results which could be disadvantageous for long term growth.

Amazon has always nearly beat Wall Street estimates on revenue but missed on profit, and this has been because of increased spending across the board, especially, marketing and shipping.

Bezos has displayed tremendous foresight and strength in defying Wall Street's expectations and anticipations for short term growth and profitability considerations, instead focusing on long term market leadership investment decisions.

Bezos has prioritized long term shareholder value instead of short term market bumps and analyst's reactions. Bezos has been clear that only market leadership can lead to higher revenues, more profitability, greater capital velocity, and correspondingly higher returns on invested capital.

His stance on market leadership exemplifies his commitment to the long term perspective.

Summary

Amazon has faced a lot of criticism for issues ranging from tax avoidance to minimum wage to Bezos' apparent lack of philanthropy. However, Bezos continues to silently work rather than get into protracted explanations regarding his action. His single absolute focus on making Amazon the most customer focused company in the world has led Amazon to develop some key precedents in all its businesses, precedents which have now become market norms. Entrepreneurs can learn a lot about customer focus, innovation and decision making from Bezos.

❑

2.
Bill Gates

Chances are your life has been touched by what this man has done.

If you have used a computer ever, Microsoft has impacted your life.

Bill Gates, the co-founder of Microsoft and its former Chairman is a business magnate, philanthropist, tech entrepreneur and investor, all rolled into one. His journey with Microsoft catapulted him into the league of the richest men in the world.

Gates has impacted a generation of computing professionals, affecting the way people work. His work at the Bill and Melinda

Gates Foundation has helped improve lives of underprivileged populations. Young entrepreneurs can learn a lot from Gates' tenacity and entrepreneurial spirit.

Gates developed an early interest in computing, and along with his friends, formed the Lakeside Programmers Club, at Lakeside school, a private institution which he attended. Gates was a brilliant scholar, scoring a 1590 out of 1600 in his SATs and eventually enrolling in Harvard in 1973.

He read up about the Altair 8800 in a magazine, sensed a business opportunity, dropped out of Harvard, and incorporated Microsoft soon after. The company achieved one milestone after another, right from the launch of Windows 1.0 in 1985, the launch of the X-Box in 2001. In 2016, Microsoft was the world's largest software company by revenue. In 2020, Microsoft was ranked 21 in the 2020 Fortune 500 rankings of the largest corporations by total revenue. It also forayed into other areas such as search by Bing, its cloud computing business (Azure) and digital services market (MSN).

Gates was the largest individual shareholder in Microsoft till 2014. He held various leadership positions during his entire tenure, including Chairman, Chief Executive Officer and Chief Software Architect – while acting as the technology advisor when Satya Nadella was appointed as the CEO.

In 2000, Gates founded the charitable foundation, the Bill & Melinda Gates Foundation, along with his wife, Melinda Gates3. In 2008, he had moved to a part time role at Microsoft and started focusing more on the foundation. In 2015, Bill announced the formation of the Child Health and Mortality Prevention Surveillance Network (CHAMPS), a network of disease surveillance sites in developing countries, to help prevent childhood deaths3. In 2020, Gates had transitioned out of his board positions at Microsoft to focus more on his philanthropic work impacting areas like education and healthcare.

Management Lessons Learnt from Bill Gates

If any entrepreneur wants to learn about innovation, risk taking and enterprise, then Bill Gates is an entrepreneur to emulate. He has inspired millions of young entrepreneurs to build their enterprise and follow their dreams.

Enterprise

Gates had always been passionate about computing – right from an early age. He had been a prodigal computing talent in high school. Even when he enrolled at Harvard, he was passionate about starting his own business in the area of computing. In December 1974, Gates came across an issue of the magazine Popular Electronics which talked about the Altair 8800. Sensing an opportunity, Gates contacted Micro Instrumentation and Telemetry Systems (MITS) to inform them that they were working on a BASIC interpreter for the platform. Actually by then, Gates and Allen had not written a code for the Altair. The exercise was to gauge the level of interest MITS had in the project4. After a meeting with the MITS leadership team, they received a go ahead, and they toiled day and night in creating it. Since they did not have an Altair, they simulated it on other computers. MITS hired both of them and that was the beginning of Gates' journey into the world of software. MITS collapsed shortly thereafter, but Gates and Allen had already commenced their entrepreneurial journey, writing software for other computer start-ups.

Vision

"We always overestimate the change that will occur in the next two years and underestimate the change that will occur in the next 10." — Bill Gates

Gates is said to have remarkable vision and foresight into how technology could be an integral part of day-to-day life. Both Gates and Allen had a vision of an age where there would be a computer in every home – this may have sounded very futuristic during their time, but it soon became a reality, with computers becoming ubiquitous and inextricably linked to our lives.

For the team members of quick growth start-up, it is sometimes difficult to understand the vision and the urgency of a founder. It is important for the founder/s to have a clear vision which can help everyone align to the organization's overall objectives. By highlighting how every team member's role contributes to the overall vision of the organization, founders can highlight the importance and uniqueness of a particular role, and onboard employees as partners and true contributors in the growth of the organization.

Inspiring Commitment

Visionary founders are also known to be great communicators – they communicate their vision, the organization's mission very clearly and often – to drive alignment.

To get people to be excited about working and earn their commitment, it is important to showcase the possibilities of a shared future, and their role in making it happen. Clarity in communication is extremely important when working towards a shared goal. Gates is known to have rallied everyone around his vision, driving his employees desire to create a remarkable future for the organization as well as themselves.

Learning from Failures

All of us have experienced failure of some kind in our lives. Entrepreneurs have channelled their failures into learning experiences. Gates is said to have remarked that success is a lousy teacher – as it lulls us into a false sense of comfort and security.

Failure presents an opportunity to evaluate ourselves, learn how to respond to a crisis, up-level ourselves, develop empathy and the ability to adapt and move forward. Companies and individuals who proactively spend time in learning from their failures are much better at responding to crisis and sudden adverse events.

Microsoft missed the bus on quite a few opportunities – one such being search. Google was founded in 1998, when Microsoft was reigning its domain. Google's complete dominance of the search engine market, and of the open-source ecosystem lead Gates to admit that Microsoft had misjudged the potential of these two opportunities.

Humanitarian Work

One of Gates's lasting legacies will be his work with the Foundation. His philosophy and vision have very clearly contributed to making the Bill and Melinda Gates Foundation to become one of the largest private foundation in the world, having over $46.9 billion in assets. Under Gates's stewardship, the foundation has done phenomenal work in expanding access to healthcare, education, and access to informational technology.

Perseverance

In the 1990s, the US government sued Microsoft for monopolistic practices in the personal computing industry. The case received a lot of press coverage and continued to dominate headlines for quite some time.

The federal agency soon ended its investigation. However, it was brought up again by the U.S. Department of Justice (DoJ) in 1998 when it filed antitrust charges against the software company.

The company was accused of bundling additional programs into its operating system. The Windows operating system became a gateway for accessing a particular Microsoft application. At the same time, Microsoft distributed its browser software, Internet Explorer (IE), among its consumers, for free. This led to rapid expansion in market share, and the eventual market share erosion for its closest competitor, Netscape. The DoJ's investigated if Microsoft was intentionally creating barriers for consumers to install third party software on personal computers that used an MS operating system6.

In 2011, after a prolonged 21-year battle in the courts, the case finally received closure, after multiple deliberations. It was an exhausting time for Gates, but he persevered in keeping the company's vision and focus intact, which is the trait of great leaders.

It is difficult to preserve in the face of litigation, negative press and uncertainty, but a true leader believes in looking forward, not being fazed by any adversities.

Constant Innovation

As a leader, understanding the market is of immense importance. Gates was constantly evaluating the changing market trends and evaluating product-market fit. Gates was aware that to maintain the leadership position in the software market, Microsoft had to constantly reinvent itself, moving from just software packages for Office to a web browser to contemporary enterprise solutions. He was instrumental in developing and creating that need for innovation and product market fit in the employees of Microsoft.

Valuing time

Gates is known to be fastidious about time, and apparently, he does not believe in postponing or deferring things for later. In an interview with Charlie Rose, where he was interviewed with Warren Buffet, Gates is said to have remarked that time is the only commodity that money cannot buy.

Young entrepreneurs can certainly learn effective time management from Gates. One of the most efficient ways of managing time is called Timeboxing, where a specific amount of time is set apart for doing particular tasks. This will certainly help entrepreneurs manage their executive time bandwidth.

Summary

For all his failings, Gates remains an epitome of innovation, hard work, and determination. Gates' vision, passion for computing, and focus helped shape Microsoft for the multi-billion-dollar enterprise that it is today.

Despite the challenges he faced—anti-trust litigation, severe competition, he steered Microsoft ably for many years, heralding a true age of computing. His humanitarian work through the Gates Foundation should inspire many other entrepreneurs to give back to society through philanthropy.

❑

3.
Steve Jobs

He has been the torchbearer of American innovation and entrepreneurship in the past few decades.

His innovation and vision have led to the transformation of nearly seven industries: personal computing, music, phones, animated movies, tablet computing, retail stores, and digital publishing.

Yet Steve Jobs remained surprisingly austere and critical in the quest for perfection.

Steve Jobs cofounded Apple from the garage of his parents in 1976, was evicted from the company in 1985, returned to its helm in 1997 and consequentially built it to become one of the most innovative and valuable enterprises in the world.

Early years

Steven Jobs was born in 1955 in San Francisco, California. Adopted at birth by Paul and Clara Jobs, Steve's family moved to Mountain View a couple of years later. His friendship with Stephen Wozniak during his adolescence paved the foundation for a lasting partnership and the creation of Apple, Inc·.

Upon graduation, Steve attended Reed College but spent only one semester there. He began working at Atari and around that time undertook a trip to India along with friends1,2. Upon his return, he renewed his friendship with Wozniak, who at that point of time was trying to build a computer. Jobs grasped the potential of what Wozniak was working on and persuaded him to partner with him to launch Apple in 1975. They began working on the prototype of the Apple I, and spent assembling boards of Apple I computers in Steve's garage, and selling them to independent computer dealers in the area·.

Around the same time, Jobs started seeking venture capital. Mike Markkula, a former Intel executive turned investor, invested nearly $250,000 in January 1977.

In 1977, the Apple II was introduced, launching the era of the personal computer, and generating $3 million in sales, increasing to $200 million two years later2. Their nascent success however hit a wall. In 1980, sales plateaued, and Apple faced stiff competition from IBM. The Apple Macintosh was introduced in 1984. It had some category defining features such as graphical-user interface controlled by a mouse and tremendous of ease-of-use2. But by this time, Jobs ran into problems with the board of directors and was evicted from the company by then CEO, John Sculley. Jobs eventually sold his shares of Apple stock and resigned in 1985.

With the funds available from a stock sale, Jobs launched NeXT, with the intention of launching a breakthrough computing device which would revolutionise higher education and research. Feature rich, and ripe with innovation, the NeXT computer, launched in 1988 had a faster processing speed, exceptional graphics and an optical disk drive. But it was priced prohibitively at $9,950. Jobs began devoting more time to Pixar around then, which he had acquired from George Lucas in 1986.

Jobs then helped create the first ever computer animated feature film, Toy Story. It took nearly four years to develop and was a runaway success when released in 1995. Buoyed by Toy Story's success, Jobs guided Pixar towards a public listing in 1996, and by virtue of his 80% stake in the company, he became a billionaire1,2.

During this time, Apple was struggling with finding focus and languished due to management apathy. Apple then acquired NeXT for $400 million and re-appointed Jobs to the board of directors as an advisor to Apple chairman and CEO Gil Amelio.

Since then, Jobs launched several transformative innovative products which forever changed the face of the American consumer products industry through products such as iMac, iPod, iPod Nano, Apple Stores, iTunes Store, MacBook, iPad, iPhone.

Jobs was diagnosed with a pancreatic neuroendocrine tumour in 2003. He died of respiratory arrest related to the tumour at the age of 56 on October 5, 2011. His contribution to the world of technological advancements remains unparalleled.

Management Lessons Learnt from Steve Jobs

Vision

Right from spotting the potential of the first computer that Wozniack built, Steve was great at understanding how technology could integrate and enhance the quality of life. His understanding of industrial design, consumer needs and required products was superlative.

Right from the launch of Apple, Jobs had envisioned a future with computers on every worker's desk, where technology was a tool in improving productivity.

At that time, Jobs had also predicted that the use of computers would rise and eventually, people would buy them for connecting into a communications network, what we know today as the internet.

Focus

In 1997, Apple was producing a wide array of computers and accessories. Upon his return to Apple, Steve saw that the focus of the company was all over, and the resulting disarray was evident in the products, the marketing and overall, the company strategy4. He narrowed down the company's focus to two segments, consumer and enterprise, and two types of products, desktop and portable and asked the teams to focus on producing one great product for each category.

Deciding what not to do is as important as deciding what to do.

Using the above framework, he redirected Apple's investment and resources towards the products that would push its revenues up.

Entrepreneurs can definitely imbibe this quality from Jobs – instead of trying to do everything, it makes much more sense to specialize in areas in which we are competitively placed.

Simplification

Jobs's design aesthetics and love of simplicity fueled an industrial design revolution. He was obsessive about simplicity, feeling that products had to be almost intuitive in their use and design. Jobs had two enduring partnerships to foster innovative design – in the 1980s with Hartmut Esslinger and then with Jonathan Ive in 1997. With these creative partnerships, Jobs created a design and engineering aesthetic that clearly helped Apple cut the clutter and become one of the most valuable enterprises in the world.

Some of the innovations that Apple helped create became the industry standard such as the rectangular design, pinch and zoom display, a multi-touch, and grid display of apps.

Anticipating Consumers Needs

Steve's maxim was to skate where the puck is going to be.

Steve had an unerring sense of what would be the next in-demand product or service from the consumer. He is said to have a better understanding of what consumers wanted, more than the consumers themselves. Steve's ability to extrapolate future customer needs profitably led Apple to dominate certain industries such as digital music sales (through the iPod and iTunes Store).

Innovation

Steve Jobs was an innovator, but with a difference. He himself did not invent anything, but made such fundamental improvements in existing technologies that they became the next market standard. Driven primarily by the user experience and design, he was the ultimate icon of inventiveness and applied imagination.

Jobs transformed every industry where Apple launched a product, whether it was personal computing, music, phones, animated movies, tablet computing, retail stores, or digital publishing.

Apple was not the pioneer in many of these industries, but the product launched by Apple definitely was the best in its category.

User Experience

Apple is the pioneer when it comes to user experience. Whether it is the iPhone or the iPod or the iPad, the products are designed to deliver delight to the customers. Every bit of hardware, every component, was thoughtfully used and complemented the overall functioning. Apple's model of integrated hardware and software helped them deliver a superlative user experience.

Failures

Steve showed remarkable resilience in bouncing back from failures. During this time, from 1985 to 1996, Jobs was involved in two big deals; the first of which was an investment. In 1986, Jobs purchased a controlling stake in a company called Pixar from George Lucas. The second one was an investment in NeXT. These were high performance machines with a sophisticated operating system. NeXT proved to be a good investment of Steve's time as around the same time Apple was looking to replace its operating system and bought NeXT in 1996, giving Steve the opportunity to come back to Apple.

Jobs also helped to turn around Pixar, helping them create the first ever computer animated feature film, Toy Story, which was an immense success when released in 1995. Jobs navigated Pixar towards a public listing in 1996, and by virtue of his 80% stake in the company, he became a billionaire.

Steve did not give up despite losing control of the company he founded, despite being evicted by the board. He quickly moved towards his next venture and gave them his full attention and needless to say, both were a success.

Likewise, entrepreneurs should learn never to give up despite their failures.

Summary

Steve Jobs has been a towering inspirational figure for entrepreneurs everywhere. His vision, ability to anticipate customer's demands, focus on user experience and simplicity earned him the status of an icon. Even though he was a remarkably tough leader, he is remembered for leading the resurgence of American innovation.

❑

4.

Jack Ma

Jack Ma is a Chinese entrepreneur, the co-founder and former executive chairman of Alibaba Group, a multinational, technology conglomerate.

Ma has been symbolic of the rise and resurgence of Chinese internet entrepreneurs, creating jobs and fuelling the growth of the Chinese economy. His net worth as on April 2021 was $51.5 billion, giving Ma the distinction of being the third-wealthiest person in China and the 27th wealthiest person in the world as ranked by the Bloomberg Billionaires Index.

Before we look at Ma's meteoric rise, lets quickly have a look at the Chinese e-commerce market. China is the world's largest ecommerce market, with 710 million people shopping digitally2. A huge chunk, nearly 76%, of digital shopping is done by people in the age group 18 – 44. Nearly 64% of the internet population engages in online commerce, pushing the online spending to around $1.1 trillion in 2020.

Jack Ma sits at the cusp of the Chinese internet commerce revolution, being the founder and the Executive Chairman of the Alibaba Group, which is the holding company with nine major subsidiaries: Alibaba.com, Tmall, Alipay, Taobao Marketplace, eTao, Alibaba Cloud Computing, Juhuasuan, 1688.com, and AliExpress.com, having a footprint in commerce, logistics and finance.

Jack Ma's story has as much resilience as fortitude, as much faith as perseverance, and serves as a dose of heady inspiration to countless entrepreneurs everywhere.

Early years

Jack Ma was born as Ma Yun on October 15, 1964, in Hangzhou, located in the south-eastern part of China. After Nixon's visit to Hangzhou in 1972, it became a popular tourist destination4. When Ma was a teenager, he became interested in learning English. Around the same time, Ma started using opportunities to improve his English. Waking up at 5:00 AM morning, and riding nearly 27 km, he frequented the town's international hotel and waited there for tourists. He offered to show them around the city as a travel guide, in return learning English from them.

Ma knew that education would be his way to a better life, but he struggled to attend college. He failed the entrance exam for the Hangzhou Teachers College twice, eventually passing in the third try. He graduated in 1988 with a Bachelor of Arts in English. After graduation, he became a lecturer in English and international trade at Hangzhou Dianzi University.

During a trip to the US in 1995, he was captivated by the internet and its impact. His first business was in the area of translation, called Hope Translation. After the translation business, he launched China Pages4. However, both businesses failed to get significant traction.

Excited by the possibility of an internet enabled business, in 1999, he quit and found Alibaba along with 18 of his friends from Hangzhou. Alibaba was then a China-based business-to-business marketplace site. The site allowed exporters to post product listings that customers could buy directly. By 1999, the firm had raised $5 million from Goldman Sachs and $20 million from SoftBank. In 2005, Yahoo invested $1 billion in Alibaba for a 40% stake in the company. This investment provided a timely fillip to Alibaba, it was engaged in a massive battle with eBay at the time for market share.

In 2003, Alibaba launched Taobao. Around the same time, eBay had acquired Eachnet, which was the dominant auction platform in China at that time for a sum of USD $180 million. eBay's might combined with the auction platform, made it a major contender in the exploding Chinese consumer e-commerce market.

Jack had devised an intense strategy to counter eBay's expansion in the China market. Right from offering free listings to introduction of instant messaging between the buyers and sellers, Taobao had its pulse on the consumers' needs. Within two years, Taobao unseated eBay and grew to have dominant market share, growing from 8% to 59% between 2003 and 2005, while eBay China's market shared dropped from 79% to 36%. Eventually, eBay shut down its Chinese site in 2006.

Alibaba notched up one milestone after another, getting listed on the Hong Kong stock exchange in 2007, went public with a $25 billion IPO.

In 2008, Tmall was introduced as a dedicated B2C platform, the key differentiator being that Tmall is a Business-to-Consumer (B2C) platform but Taobao is Consumer to Consumer (C2C). Tmall.com eventually became the largest B2C retail platform in Asia, becoming the entry point for businesses looking for a China retail strategy and an important avenue for Chinese market penetration.

In 2004, Ma launched Alipay, which eventually overtook PayPal as the world's largest mobile payment platform in 20137. In 2018, the number of Alipay users surpassed a staggering 870 million.

Alibaba continues to grow at a frenetic pace, despite challenges. Though Ma transitioned out as Chairman a few years ago, his leadership, vision and drive continue to impact Alibaba every day.

Management Lessons Learnt from Jack Ma

Embracing Rejection

One continuing theme in Jack Ma's success is his ability to embrace rejection and move beyond it. Despite failing twice in the college examinations, he attempted it a third time, eventually passing. After not being selected by KFC upon its China entry, he did not lose hope. In one interview, he remarked upon his rejection from Harvard Business School. Despite repeated rejections, Jack Ma did not give up.

Jack has no Ivy League education, had very few connections prior to his Alibaba days, and had scant mathematical proficiency, things typically considered to be enablers for a successful business. Yet, Jack embraced these rejections and setbacks, acknowledged them, and through his success and his work, they ceased to matter.

Ambition

Jack is supposed to have stated "We don't want to be number one in China. We want to be number one in the world."

Jack was very clear about the global impact that he wanted Alibaba to make, and he has repeated this message right from Alibaba's early days.

On the eve of Alibaba's 18th birthday, at a celebration in Hangzhou, he is said to have remarked "Alibaba is already the world's 21th largest economic entity today. In another 19 years, we aim to make Alibaba the world's 5th largest economic entity. We hope to provide 100 million jobs around the world, serve 2 billion consumers, and create a profit platform for 10 million small and medium enterprises."

This is just a snapshot of his grand vision for Alibaba, which has inspired entrepreneurs across the world.

Resilience

In 2007, eBay was focused on extracting more market share in China. eBay obviously had more financial reserves than the young start-up which Jack helmed.

However, Jack played to his strengths.

He handpicked a team which started working on Taobao, and believed in taking the fight to eBay6. Taobao was launched with much fanfare, announcing that it would be free for the first three years, a direct attack on eBay, which collected fees from its users. His deep understanding of the Chinese market, supplemented by his knowledge of consumers, understood that in China, trust was a key factor. The free for three years strategy was just a starter.

Taobao became the market leader in China within three years of its launch, growing its market share from 8% to 59% between 2003 and 20056. At the same time, eBay's market share dropped from 79% to 36%, eventually forcing eBay to shut down its Chinese site in 2006.

Unorthodox Leadership

Ma's leadership style is said to be quite unorthodox, belying the expectations Wall Street analysts. In his transitioning out ceremony, he signed off as The Executive Chairman of Alibaba Group by appearing onstage as a reggae-rock star while singing. On the eve of Alibaba's 18th birthday, Ma appeared onstage dressed up in a costume and entertained Alibaba employees by performing dance moves inspired by Michael Jackson.

All this makes for his unique leadership style, endearing him to his employees, further adding to his charisma.

Vision

Jack's vision for Alibaba is what propelled a nascent start-up into supersonic growth. Right from the very beginning, he was clear that Alibaba's competitors were not Chinese companies but rather global companies. He stated that he wanted Alibaba to be around for a long time, around 100+ years, spanning three centuries. He has always exhorted his team to think bigger and act timely.

He has continuously expanded Alibaba's global ambition stating that he would like the company to generate half its sales from outside China by 2025. In his final speech before transitioning out as the Chairman, he stated that "In the next 20 years, our mission is to make the best use of resources, talent, technology, in order for the world to be greener, more equal and sustainable," laying the foundation of Alibaba's vision for the next 20 years.

He is largely credited with the resurgence of retail, coining the word, New Retail. He infused similar energy in manufacturing, often seen as an old-world industry by urging manufacturers to embrace and incorporate these new technologies to keep up with changing consumption trends. New Manufacturing, as Ma envisions it, integrates emerging technology such as data, artificial intelligence, cloud computing and the internet of things and weaves it seamlessly in the manufacturing process, making it current and relevant.

Summary

In an age of disdain and mistrust with the corporate world, Jack Ma comes as a refreshing change. His contribution to creating an ecosystem of Chinese entrepreneurship has led to resurgence of capitalism in China. Much loved by his employees, who treat him like a combination of father figure, mentor and leader, has led to the creation of one of the most loyal employees across any company, one unified by vision and the desire to change.

With Alibaba, Ma has built both a brand and a culture, a culture of risk taking, innovation and bold experimentation, one that is reflective of the new China.

❑

5.
Larry Page & Sergey Brin

An innocuous sounding paper.

The Anatomy of a Large-Scale Hypertextual Web Search Engine.

And this is how it all began.

With this paper, Larry Page and Sergey Brin literally launched Google, the search engine that would be the portal for any query in the world.

When Google filed for an IPO in 2004 and raised $1.7 billion, it had a valuation of $27 billion. The company has been a hotspot for innovation since it launched. It now has businesses in search, cloud computing, software, hardware and is considered to be one of the most valuable tech companies in the world. The founders, Larry and Sergey have a net worth of almost $100 billion, making them both one of the richest men in the world.

Early years

Larry was born as Lawrence Edward Page on March 26, 1973 to Carl Victor Page Sr. and Gloria Page4. Page grew up in an environment where computing was all around him. His father a computer science professor, and a pioneer in artificial intelligence, at Michigan State University. His mother was an instructor in computer programming at Lyman Briggs College. Page grew up amongst gadgets, computers, and books4. He started experimenting with computers when he was all of six years old. He received his Bachelor's education in computer engineering from the University of Michigan, and he enrolled for his Master of Science in computer science from Stanford university.

Sergey was born Sergey Mikhaylovich Brin on born August 21, 1973. The Brin family immigrated to the United States from the Soviet Union when Sergey was six. He received his Bachelor's education in mathematics and computer science at the University of Maryland. He then enrolled in in Stanford for his PhD degree.

It was at Stanford that Larry met Sergey in 1995.

Page was then exploring themes for his dissertation and was exploring the mathematical properties of the World Wide Web, understanding its link structure as a huge graph. Encouraged by his supervisor, Page began working on the problem.

Page focused on finding out how pages were interconnected with each other and the importance of backlinks. The underlying framework for the algorithm that they developed, PageRank, was the same as it was in academic publishing – well authored papers received more citations. Sergey joined in after sometime and their project was unofficially called "BackRub." It was then that they both authored the research paper "The Anatomy of a Large-Scale Hypertextual Web Search Engine", which then became one of the most downloaded scientific documents on the internet.

PageRank became the foundational algorithm of Google Search and went live on Stanford's network in 1996. In 1998, they founded Google Inc and the company has become the pioneer in major tech innovations in the past two decades.

It now has business interests in not just search, but also online advertising technologies, cloud computing, software, and hardware. It has also earned itself a place in the Internet Hall of Fame as one of the four big companies, Facebook, Amazon, and Apple.

In 2015, Google reorganized its business and Google became a wholly owned, and the largest, subsidiary of Alphabet Inc. It also became the umbrella company for Alphabet's Internet interests. Subsequently, Sundar Pichai was appointed as the CEO of Google, and Page became the CEO of Alphabet. In 2019, Pichai was appointed as the CEO of Alphabet as well.

Over the years, Google has faced backlash due to concerns around privacy, tax avoidance, search neutrality, censorship, antitrust and abuse of its monopoly position.

Management Lessons Learnt from Larry Page and Sergey Brin

Think big

Google has always prioritized big thinking – big, disruptive innovations which have the potential to change the world. Both Page and Brin believe investing in these totally audacious ideas that can have huge upsides for both the company and the world if successful. This executive level focus on disruption has steered the company from incremental innovations for small runway growth, which tend to get rewarded well by Wall Street analysts, making Google totally one of the its kind.

In 2003, when Google was just four years old, its sales hit $1.5 billion and its profit was $100 million, it had 80% market share of the search market. Since then, it has continued to completely dominate mostly all the categories where it operates, sometimes creating completely new net categories.

This moonshot thinking, advocated by Larry and Sergey, amongst a group of highly intelligent, committed and entrepreneurial employees enables on operationalising almost science fiction- like ideas that can make massive improvements in the lives of billions of people.

Employees at Google regularly ask questions like:

1 Would the solution for the problem have a transformational effect?

2. Will it produce growth of 10 percent or 10X?

Entrepreneurs can certainly learn big-scale thinking from the Google founders. Instead of investing in incremental innovations, founders should certainly work on solutions of problems which have massive impact.

Innovation

Google has had some phenomenal innovations over the years. It is this appetite for innovation that makes it an attractive talent destination, with people flocking to work on some of the most game changing projects across the globe. Many of its innovations are completely led by employees, further putting credence to their very high standards for talent acquisition.

Some innovations that Google lead and have now become ubiquitous include Google Maps, self-driving cars, Android, Google Glass, amongst others.

The company now owns a range of productivity and communication platforms – Google Docs, Google Sheets, Google Slides, email communication through Gmail, cloud storage through Google Drive, instant communication on their messaging apps and platforms (Google Duo, Google Chat, and Google Meet), translation through Google Translate, navigation through Google Maps, Waze, Google Earth, and Street View). Google also owns major content publishing platforms such as YouTube and Blogger, making it a veritable unstoppable force on the internet.

The company also lead the development of the Android mobile operating system, the Chrome browser, and Chrome OS. It also ventured into hardware with the launch of Google Nexus, Google Pixel range of smartphones. Now it has ventured into smart homes with Google Home along with driverless cars and other future looking technologies.

Google encourages employees to innovate by prioritizing projects which have a big impact and fundamentally improve the user experience by 10X. It also encourages employees to launch in beta and test and iterate.

Google has acquired many companies where they felt an acquisition could quickly help them stay ahead of the curve. One such acquisition was Page's estimation of the rise of mobile computing, and subsequently, the acquisition of a small start-up in 2005 called Android for $50 million. Android helped Google gain traction in the mobile software market.

In 2006, Google acquired YouTube for $1.65 billion in Google stock and in 2008, they acquired DoubleClick for $3.1 billion, further fortifying Google's portfolio.

The idea of 10x thinking is embedded deep within Google. The principle of innovation is that innovation has the maximum impact when it changes the outcomes by 10x rather than 10%.

Both the co-founders have instilled a deep desire of innovation within Google, and rewarded and encouraged innovation at all levels. As a result, everything that Google does, becomes category defining and ultimately category dominating.

Hiring Great Talent

Google is known for hiring the best talent – in engineering, marketing and most functions. The belief is that great people will not only help the company move forward but also act as a talent magnet for other great hires.

As per a research conducted by Bain & Company, tech companies like Apple, Google, Dell and Netflix are 40% more productive than other companies, also having correspondingly higher profit margins, ranging from 30% to 50%. The research further cites how A-level talent helps these companies maintain their competitive advantage.

Every year, Google receives millions of resumes, with a hiring ratio of less than 1%. What makes Google such as aspirational talent destination is not just its fantastic work policies and massive campuses replete with best-in-class facilities, but the chance to work with some of the smartest people in the world10. With around 140,000 employees spread across the globe, Google is on the top end of innovation, disruption and cutting edge technological changes. In terms of dollar value of productivity and profit Google's employees outrank employees from other companies by far.

It is routinely cited in the Top Places to Work index because of its phenomenal employee-development programs. Employees are encouraged to invest 20% of their worktime on new learning and self-development, further increasing the company's innovation capital. Given the work environment, the company has the highest employee retention rates across any of the companies in the world.

Entrepreneurs can learn how important it is to hire and develop the right talent. For young companies, having the correct talent in the initial phases can make a world of difference. If a company is known as a good workplace and is known to hire people of high calibre, it will automatically get sought after as a high-end talent destination, will see lower attrition. Employees will also be motivated and happy and will be more productive.

Summary

Larry Page and Sergey Brin have inarguably built the most innovative and one of the most profitable companies in the world. Their focus on innovation, moonshot thinking and hiring the right talent to build a world class enterprise is certainly something that all entrepreneurs can emulate.

❑

6.
Elon Musk

Think of all the transformative changes taking place in society today.

- Electric cars
- Space exploration
- Transportation
- Payments

There is one man whose bold vision has helped create enterprises of the future Elon Musk; CEO and CTO of SpaceX; CEO & chief product architect of Tesla Motors; Chairman of SolarCity, and co-founder of PayPal; Hyperloop; And many more.

Not since Steve Jobs has an American entrepreneur captured popular imagination so completely like Musk. Whether he is being a hard-nosed entrepreneur, or the liberal do-gooder, Musk is like the poster child of unconventional decisions, decisions which seemed crazy many years ago, but have only enhanced his net worth in the past few.

According to the Bloomberg Billionaires Index, he has an estimated total net worth of $209 billion, surpassing Jeff Bezos as the richest person in the world, as of January 2021.

This story is not just about Musk's tremendous entrepreneurial spirit and innovation but also about how he almost went broke along the way, was plied with lawsuits, invited government censure scrutiny, and became one of the most loved and most controversial figures in the world of business, simultaneously.

What we learn from Musk's never say die entrepreneurial spirit is the ability to turn every adversity into opportunity, and to have a relentless drive to succeed.

Elon Reeve Musk was born on June 28, 1971, in Pretoria, South Africa. His father, Errol Musk, is a British engineer born in South Africa. His mother, Maye Musk is Canadian-English and a dietetics expert. At the age of 9, Musk got his first personal computer, the Commodore VIC-20. Hooked to programming, he learnt it all by himself and at the age of 12, made his first sale by earning $500 by creating and selling a computer game he developed called Blastar. Right from that young age, Musk's ambition to succeed is a driving force that young entrepreneurs might want to emulate.

Musk completed his education in Canada and the US, attending the Queen's University in Kingston, Ontario, till 1992. Two years later, he transferred to the University of Pennsylvania, Philadelphia, and graduated in 1997 with a dual degree in physics and economics. He enrolled in the PhD program at Stanford

University in California in 1995, but he left after only two days to explore the potential of an internet start-up. His risk taking appetite was legendary, and this was just the start of the entrepreneurial journey of a lifetime.

Zip2 & PayPal

In 1995, with an investment of $28,000 in partnership with his younger brother, Kimbal Musk, Musk launched his first venture, Zip2, a web software company that would help newspapers develop online city guides.

In 1999, Zip2 was acquired by Compaq's AltaVista web search engine for a stunning $340 million, and marked Elon's entrance into the million dollar entrepreneur club.

Elon then proceeded towards his next venture X.com, with which he planned a disruptive product in the banking industry. X merged with another company called Confinity and merged company is what we know as PayPal. Musk was then ousted from the company before it was bought by eBay for $1.5 billion.

Tesla

One of Musk's ventures, Tesla, is an electric vehicle and clean energy company based in Palo Alto, California. Tesla's current products include electric cars, battery energy storage from home to grid scale, solar panels and solar roof tiles, as well as other related products and services.

Tesla was founded by entrepreneurs Martin Eberhard and Marc Tarpenning. Musk participated in the Series A round of investments in 2004, joining Tesla's board of directors as its chairman. At that time, Musk was involved in overall product design but was not deeply involved in day-to-day business operations. Subsequent to a series of conflicts, Eberhard was ousted from the firm, with Musk taking up leadership responsibilities as company CEO and product architect in 2008. In 2009 a lawsuit settlement with

Eberhard designated Musk as a Tesla co-founder, along with Tarpenning and two others.

The first Tesla product, the Roadster, was launched with a prototype display in 2006, which could travel 245 miles (394 km) on a single charge. Unlike the prevalent electric vehicles existing in the market at that time, the Roadster was like a sports car that could accelerate from 0 to 60 miles (97 km) per hour in less than four seconds.

Tesla's IPO in 2010 enabled the company to raise about $226 million. In 2012, Tesla launched the Model S sedan. The performance and design of Model S was highly appreciated by automotive critics. The company won further acclaim for its Model X luxury SUV, which was launched in 2015. In 2017, The Model 3, a less expensive vehicle, went into production. In 2019, the company launched Cybertruck, an all-electric pickup truck. In 2020, the company launched the Model Y crossover and also hit the milestone of producing 1 million electric cars.

SpaceX

SpaceX is an American aerospace manufacturer and space transportation services provider12. Founded in 2002, with an investment of $100 million of Musk's early fortune, it had the mission of launching affordable space transportation and space colonization12. Since its inception, SpaceX has developed several launch vehicles and rocket engines, as well as the Dragon cargo spacecraft and the Starlink satellite constellation (providing internet access), and has enabled the transportation of humans and cargo to the International Space Station (ISS) on the SpaceX Dragon 2.

After three failed launches, SpaceX succeeded in launching the Falcon 1 in 2008. It was the first private liquid-fuel rocket to reach the Earth's orbit. In 2012, it became the first private company to launch a spacecraft to the ISS13. In 2018, SpaceX had over 100 launches on its manifest representing about US$12 billion in contract revenue. In 2019, it became the first private company to autonomously dock a spacecraft to the ISS. In May 2020, SpaceX achieved a valuation of USD $36 billion, subsequently increasing to USD $46 billion in August 2020 to $74 billion in 2021.

Hyperloop

Musk went on from embracing one disruptive area to next.

In August 2013, Musk unveiled to the world, what would be another ground breaking innovation – a new form of transportation called the "Hyperloop," an invention that would enable faster commuting between major cities15. Powered by renewable energy, resistant to weather, the Hyperloop would propel riders in pods through a network of low-pressure tubes at speeds reaching more than 700 mph. Musk shared that the Hyperloop could take 7-10 years to be built.

Although Hyperloop estimated costs were around $6 billion — approximately one-tenth of the cost for the rail system planned by the state of California — Musk's ideas were met with scepticism. The projected cost of a high-speed rail system in California, were around $68 billion. Hyperloop's pneumatic tubes, carrying 28 passengers, would travel the 350 miles (560 km) between Los Angeles and San Francisco in 35 minutes at a top speed of 760 miles (1,220 km) per hour, nearly the speed of sound. Musk's claims that the Hyperloop's projected costs ($6 billion) and frequency (pods departing every two minutes on average) would enable around six million people to travel that route every year.

Last known, with this hands full with SpaceX and Tesla, Musk has not been able to devote more time to the Hyperloop's development.

OpenAI & Neuralink

Like other inventors, Musk has a keen interest in artificial intelligence and is of the view that Artificial General Super intelligences (AGSIs) will present an enormous existential risk to humanity's future on Earth. He is the co-founder of the non-profit, OpenAI, which provides free access to its advanced AI research results. The research company commenced operations in 2015 with the mission of advancing digital intelligence to benefit humanity, and disseminating techniques for making AGSI safe, and to prevent powerful groups from monopolizing AGSI.

In 2017, it was also reported that Musk was backing a venture called Neuralink, a neurotechnology start up, which would focus on integration of human systems with artificial intelligence. He expanded on the company's progress during a July 2019 discussion, unveiling plans that might include integrable devices such as microscopic chips connecting to a smartphone via bluetooth. Reputed scientific publications such as the MIT Technology Review have described these claims as "highly speculative" and "neuroscience theatre."

The Boring Company

In January 2017, Musk launched The Boring Company, an infrastructure and tunnel construction services company. TBC commenced with a test dig on the SpaceX property in Los Angeles.

In 2018, Musk confirmed that he would cover the estimated $1 billion needed to dig the 17-mile tunnel from the airport to downtown Chicago, solving a major city transportation problem. In May 2019, TBC acquired a $48.7 million contract from the Las Vegas Convention and Visitors Authority to build an underground Loop system to shuttle people around the Las Vegas Convention Center. Subsequently, in the same year, Musk announced on Twitter that TBC would first focus on completing the first commercial tunnel in Las Vegas before commencing other projects.

Personal life

Musk has been married twice. He wed Justine Wilson in 2000, and have five children together: twins Griffin and Xavier (born in 2004) and triplets Kai, Saxon and Damian (born in 2006).

After an acrimonious divorce from Wilson, Musk met actress Talulah Riley. The couple married in 2010. They separated in 2012 but married each other again in 2013. Their relationship ultimately ended in divorce in 2016. In May 2018, Musk and Canadian musician Grimes revealed that they were dating and in May 2020 Grimes gave birth to their son, X Æ A-12.

Musk is a known donor to philanthropic causes, be it the Giving Pledge or donations to non-profits. In October 2019 Musk pledged to donate $1 million to the #TeamTrees campaign, which aims to plant 20 million trees around the world by 2020.

Management Lessons Learnt from Musk

Musk's abstract and parallel thought process, along with his risk taking spirit and never say die attitude are all traits to emulate for young entrepreneurs.

Musk has repeatedly taken on high risk projects, which have later on shown to have tremendous dividends, and have become category defining innovations. His commitment to systems change and creating a future that is inspiring and appealing is worth emulating. He does not let existing obstructions and infrastructure impede his functioning.

His ability to take on big audacious goals, and define concrete business strategies from abstract concepts is one of his strengths. Driven by a desire to accomplish big things, right from inspiring the world to changing the way it consumes natural resources to leveraging artificial and human intelligence, Musk finds purpose in trying to drive humanity forward.

One of the classic traits that leaders should have is the ability to adapt and pivot – and Musk displays this amply. Right from the initial failures of SpaceX, Musk spent years trying, failing, and learning from all the failures and quick pivots, ultimately leading to success.

Large organizations tend to become comfortable with status-quo. Changing the organizational course of action abruptly as a leader can be disorienting for the rest of the team. But a leader needs to take bold, unprecedented moves. No one has displayed this more strongly than Musk, having disrupted every single category he entered.

However, Elon Musk is not a perfect, infallible role model. He is an innovator par excellence, but is known to be volatile and of erratic temper. Despite his extraordinary vision and capability, he is an incredibly hard man to work for. He regularly works 80-hour weeks, and he expects his employees to contribute similarly.

His philosophy, science fiction, physics and fantasy novels are reflected in his sense of idealism and the companies in which he has invested. His concerns around artificial intelligence, around human existence, renewable energy and have all led to pushing the frontiers in creating the companies of tomorrow – be it PayPal, Tesla Motors, SolarCity, SpaceX, Hyperloop, and The Boring Company, defining innovation for generations to come.

❑

7.
Mark Zuckerberg

It is probably the company that has singularly received love and hate in equal measure.

Its leadership has been part of Senate committee hearings and has been charged with numerous charges from inciting hate speech to cyber-bullying, to the rising incidents of mental health issues, election integrity, privacy, and data portability, and teen suicide rates.

It has been the subject of intense scrutiny and cynosure and has been under the lens of lawmakers for a long time.

Yet, when in 2004, its Founder, 19-year-old Mark Zuckerberg, launched it from his dorm room along with four of his friends, it was very different from what it is today.

Launched as "thefacebook.com" in Kirkland House at Harvard University, it was initially just a social networking platform. Today, Facebook is a media behemoth, having moved beyond social networking to a messaging app to a mega monolith, having acquired Instagram, WhatsApp, Oculus VR, Giphy and Mapillary.

Born in May 1984 in New York, Zuckerberg's father, Edward, is a dentist, and his mother, Karen is a psychiatrist. Zuckerberg has three other siblings, sisters, Randi, Donna, and Arielle4. His is widely regarded as a childhood programming prodigy having worked on computing programs and building games and applications much before Facebook, such as Zucknet (we will learn about this later in this chapter), CourseMatch (a program that allowed users to make class selection decisions based on the peer decisions, also allowing them to form study groups), followed by Facemash, a peer ranking program developed while he was in Harvard, which received intense backlash.

Facebook's inception is shrouded in litigation as well, with accusations that Zuckerberg stole an idea from his Harvard peers, twins Cameron and Tyler Winklevoss, and Divya Narendra, who were then working on the social network idea called HarvardConnection.com.

Facebook grew outside of Harvard, enlisting student population from other universities, Columbia, Stanford, Yale, and Brown, ultimately reaching the 500 million user mark in July 2010. Facebook filed for an IPO on February 1, 2012, having around 845 million active users at that time. Since that time, Facebook has acquired Instagram, Onavo, WhatsApp, and Giphy amongst others.

In July 2019, Facebook was the subject of an anti-trust investigation launched by the Federal Trade Commission (FTC). Over time, Facebook's advertising revenue has grown and the company has facing increasing accusations about data privacy, harmful content and cyber bullying, none of which can seemingly stop the growth of the company that Mark started from his dorm room.

Management Lessons Learnt from Zuckerberg

Innovation

Zuckerberg had been a programming prodigy, having received private coaching for it early in his childhood. In his pre-teens, Zuckerberg developed,"ZuckNet", a communications platform that allowed all the computers between the house and dental office in his father's dental practice to communicate with each other. When he was in high school, he worked in the Intelligent Media Group to build a music player called the Synapse Media Player. It harvested machine learning to learn the user's listening habits.

Zuckerberg was a passionate inventor, continuously generating inventions that he felt were communication enablers. His innovation capacity is an important driver for Facebook's early growth.

Quick Decision Making

Until 2014, Facebook's motto was "Move Fast and Break Things." It meant that the new developments, features might not be perfect, but the ideation and creation were important, with speed being the primary driver. This motto perfectly captures Facebook's decision making ideology in the beginning, that speed and creation were important.

Often times in entrepreneurship, business owners are conflicted with decision making, not being able to make decisions, thus affecting their ability to scale and expand their business.

Entrepreneurs can learn quick decision making from Zuckerberg, albeit after weighing in the outcomes of each decisions carefully.

Vision

In recent years, Zuckerberg has become more participative in influencing and changing the global business landscape. He is known to champion the cause of democratizing internet access, raising this issue even at his address at the United Nations. Zuckerberg has said that internet access is crucial in developing nations, helping people to protect human rights and highlight social issues. He has continuously engaged with heads of states for sharing his vision tackling various global social problems.

Handling Criticism

Facebook has been accused of propagating harmful content, compromising election integrity, privacy, and questions around data portability. It has been the subject of numerous lawsuits and investigations, across the globe.

Whether it has been the recent incident in Australia involving news media or the 2020 anti-trust lawsuit launched by the FTC and 46 states of the United States, Facebook has always been under the scanner. The 2020 lawsuit expressed concern over Facebook's acquisition of Instagram and WhatsApp – virtually creating a monopolistic market.

Zuckerberg has always taken things in his stride and has steadfastly focused on Facebook's growth. Young entrepreneurs when faced with adversity can take a leaf of out Mark's handling of the various investigations and learn how to handle business crises with equanimity.

Summary

By no means is Zuckerberg completely exonerated of the various allegations and criticisms he faces – some of the charges are quite serious. But it is commendable to see someone launching a company at 19, learning to transition to a leadership role, and trying to fix the problems of the company that has grown so much more than a simple social media networking platform.

❑

8.
Jack Dorsey

Recently, a certain tweet was in the news – for being valued at an auction at almost 2.9 million USD.

The said tweet was the first tweet on the microblogging platform, Twitter, by its Founder, Jack Dorsey, who plans to convert the proceeds from its NFT auction to bitcoin and donate them for charity.

In the world of crazy valuations received by tech companies, Twitter was one of the very firsts.

In his entire association with Twitter, he has been the CEO, executive chairman and chairman of the board. For a brief duration he did not occupy the position of CEO in 2008; he returned to resume the position in 2015. In 2009, Dorsey partnered with Jim McKelvey to launch Square, which went public in 2015. Let us have a look at the journey of this tech titan.

Born in Missouri, Dorsey's parents are Tim and Marcia. By the time Dorsey was 14, he had developed an interest in dispatch routing. While in still in his teens, Dorsey created a software that was to become the backbone of taxi-dispatch services. Despite enrolling in University of Missouri – Rolla, with a subsequent transfer to New York University in 1997, Jack never finished college. Along the same time, he became interested in instant messaging as an area. Eventually, his refined his idea and along with Evan Williams, Biz Stone, and Noah Glass founded the parent company – the Obvious Corporation – and eventually Twitter in 20063. Dorsey posted the first Twitter message on March 21, 2006 (the very same tweet which is being auctioned now for 2.9 million USD1. Twitter was launched as a microblogging and social networking service, restricted to 140 characters, eventually doubled to 280 characters in 2017.

Twitter continued to see growth as a microblogging platform, gaining popularity and users.

Twitter exploded on the scene in the South by Southwest Interactive (SXSWi) conference held in 2007. During the event duration, Twitter's tweet volume went up from 20,000 tweets to 60,000 tweets per day. The app hit 400,000 tweets per quarter in 2007, which hit another stratospheric high in 2008, with around 100 million tweets. In March 2011, Twitter had a record 140 million tweets posted daily. Usage spiked around major sporting events, with product enhancements happening in the background.

In 2009, Dorsey entered the payments space with his new venture, Square, which he cofounded. Square offered devices and software to facilitate credit-card transactions. By 2012, Square had more than two million users, a testament to its acceptance by users.

Management Lessons Learnt from Jack Dorsey

1. **Bold Risk Taking:** At the time of launching Square, Jack was aware that people were waiting for the venture to fail. In a much talked about move, he listed 140 reasons why Square would fail – along with his own disagreements on the reasons, and presented it to the investors.

   Entrepreneurs can learn a lot from Dorsey's calculated risk taking. An entrepreneurs belief in his his/her own idea has to be absolute. This is one thing that Dorsey has certainly demonstrated and is worth emulating.

2. **Structure and Time Management:** Dorsey has famously structured his entire work week into functional slots. Being the CEO of two multibillion dollar companies, it is an essential management ask. Dorsey's weekly calendar looks like this:

   - Monday is reserved for addressing management issues;
   - Tuesday is blocked off for product engineering and design decisions;
   - Wednesday is set apart for growth, marketing and communications;
   - Thursday is scheduled for meetings with outside partners and developers;
   - Friday is reserved for company, culture and recruiting;
   - Saturday is a day off;
   - Sunday is for strategy discussions and job interviews.

3. **Management of Adversity:** In the follow up to the 2016 presidential election and subsequent investigations of meddling, Dorsey had to testify before the Senate Intelligence Committee alongside other tech CEOs in September 2018. The microblogging platform had faced widespread

cynosure about its role in the interference in election results and after the testimony, Twitter shares fell by six percent. However, Jack masterfully steered the testimony, openly stating facts, and sharing that "increased transparency was critical to promoting healthy public conversation on Twitter and earning trust."

Summary

In an era where social media has come under immense fire for charges ranging from cyber bullying to fake news to meddling in elections, it is not easy to lead a company that is known as the townhall of the world. Jack has led the company admirably, steering it through various crisis and challenges, and provide leadership insights for countless entrepreneurs everywhere.

❑

9.
Sam Walton

Introduction

Sam Walton is known for transforming the retail industry forever, through his discounted, customer-first retail strategy. He single handedly built Walmart into the biggest retailer in the world, while competing with behemoths like Kmart, Sears and Woolworth's in his time.

Early Years

Sam Walton was born on March 29, 1918 in Kingfisher, Oklahoma to Thomas Gibson Walton and Nancy Lee Walton1. He attended the University of Missouri and worked as a lifeguard, waiter, and newspaper delivery driver to pay for his tuition fee.

Graduating in 1940, with a degree in economics, he wanted to attend the Wharton School of Business at the University of Pennsylvania, but had to let go of his dream as he couldn't afford the tuition fee.

He began his career in retail by taking up a job as a manager trainee at J.C. Penney for 18 months, before being drafted to serve in the Army during the World War II. He served as a communications officer in the Army Intelligence Corps and was released from service in 1945.

By that time, Walton had to support his wife and child and decided to pursue entrepreneurship. He put in his savings, USD 5000, and borrowed USD 20,000 from his father-in-law and purchased a Ben Franklin variety store in Arkansas at the age of 27.

Growth of Walmart

Walton created a strategy of competitive pricing and through discounting, was able to expand his business sufficiently to acquire more stores.

After his landlord refused to extend his lease, Walton searched for a new location and finally zeroed in on Bentonville, opening his Walton's Five & Dime in 1950. Though there were other stores, they were not able to compete with Walton's competitive pricing. As a result, his store did good business and Walton continued to expand by acquiring new stores, finally owning 15 stores by 1960.

Walton wanted to pursue a heavily discounted strategy by leveraging volume sales, supported by big stores with massive discounting, in small towns in America.

Walton wasn't the only entrepreneur launching discount-based retail stores. In that year, S.S. Kresge launched Kmart and Woolworth's launched Woolco, but Walton was rapidly expanding1.

Rural customers were delighted to have big retailers with massive discounts in their towns. Walmart soon grew to 18 stores throughout Arkansas and Missouri by 1969. In 1970, Walton decided to make Walmart public, and the IPO generating nearly $5 million1.

After the IPO, with the funds now available for expansion, Walmart grew rapidly, with around 276 stores by 1980. Walton soon launched Sam's Wholesale Clubs, meant for small business owners and wholesale dealers. Walmart soon grew to be the third largest retailer in the United States and Walton finally moved to the chairmanship role.

Walton passed away on April 5, 1992 in Arkansas.

Management Lessons Learnt from Sam Walton

Technology

Due to his retail experience prior to Walmart, Walton knew that keeping cost controls were essential to the business and a tight inventory control ordering system was crucial to the success of his stores. Walton was obsessed with maintaining inventory track records, anticipating demand and filling out back-orders. It wasn't a surprise when Walmart was one of the first major retailers to install electronic scanners at cash registers linked to a central inventory-control computer.

Walmart embraced technology much before its competitors. It adopted UPC barcodes to automate the inventory process in 1980s. In 1983, Walmart invested in a private satellite system that could track delivery trucks, speed credit card transactions, and transmit audio and video signals and sales data. It has continually invested in technology since, using it to stay ahead of its competitors.

Employee Welfare

Walton referred to his employees as associates and also undertook profit sharing with some employees, and also provided them stock options. Associates also managed their own departments, managing stock and profits2. However, in the years after Walton's death, Walmart received a lot of scrutiny and criticism about ill-treatment of employees, low wages, making employees work overtime without pay and so on.

Supply Chain

Walton was a supply chain strategist. To optimize on inventory, Walmart stores originally were located within a day's driving distance from the company's distribution centre to ensure almost instantaneous restocking. Walmart's supply chain was famous in stock-to-sale clearance within 3 days, while paying vendors every thirty days.

Financial Prudence

Understand the Value of the Dollar

Walton was extremely frugal and despised having a flashy lifestyle. He balanced his needs of comfort and luxury with that of future savings and investments. This reflects even in Walmart's logo, Save Money, Live Better.

Entrepreneurs should certainly steer clear of lavish expenses and first work to secure the future of the company. They should learn to balance their needs with savings and investments in order to ensure that the company's prospects do not suffer.

Rebounding from Failures

Walton had received tremendous success with his first retail venture, prior to Walmart. He was the owner of a Ben Franklin variety store in Newport, Arkansas and had almost a record

$250,000 in sales and $30 - 40,000 in profit. His family had just settled in Newport but a slight mistake cost him tremendously. Eager to start his business, Walton had agreed to sharing 5% of the sales revenue with the landlord, which was quite high. He also overlooked the lease renewal clause, and the landlord exploited this, ensuring that he bought the full store, along with the inventory, fixtures and furniture, forcing Walton to leave. Though he was devastated, but he chosen to strategize and start again. He relocated to Bentonville, Arkansas, and started all over again, opening his store once again.

Entrepreneurs should surely learn how to move past rejections and failures and how to rebound back from setbacks.

Summary

Walton's legacy is not just about a retail empire but one of putting the customer first. Entrepreneurs can learn how to start on a small scale, learn from one's failures and build a colossal empire by constantly innovating to stay ahead of the competition. Walton also faced multiple failures in his life, but he did not let the setbacks discourage him from pursuing his dreams.

❑

10.
Ray Kroc

If there ever was a brand that symbolised wholesome, American goodness, it is McDonalds.

Recognized the world over, people have adopted it as one of their own. You could be anywhere in the world, but the golden arches would always symbolize the same thing: quick, hot, delicious meals.

Founded in 1940 by brothers Richard and Maurice McDonald, in San Bernardino, California, United States, McDonald's has its origins in a restaurant, later, a hamburger stand, and eventually, a franchisee chain1. Ray Kroc joined the company as a franchise agent in 1955 and eventually purchased the chain from Richard and Maurice. The sheer size of McDonald's, with an annual revenue of $19.208B in 2020, serving over 69 million customers daily in over 100 countries across 37,000 outlets, employing 1.7 million employees, confirms that McDonalds is a behemoth.

Over time, it has adapted to allegations of promoting unhealthy food, and has added healthier food options to its menu such as salads, fish, smoothies, and fruit.

McDonalds' earns its revenues from the rent, royalties, and fees paid by the franchisees, as well as sales in company-operated restaurants. It has the distinction of being of the world's largest private employers, and as of 2020, has the ninth-highest global brand valuation.

However, McDonald's history is inexorably intertwined with that of Ray Kroc. McDonald's massive expansion spree began with Kroc's purchase of the McDonald brothers' equity in the company in 1961.

Under Kroc's tenure, significant changes to the business model were made, where it acquired the land for the franchisees and rented it out to them. The company owns the land on which the restaurants are built, which is valued at an estimated $16 -$18 billion and earns a sizeable percentage of its revenue from rental payments from franchisees. These rent payments rose 26% between 2010 and 2015, accounting for one-fifth of the company's total revenue at the end of the period.

Management Lessons Learnt from Ray Kroc

If any entrepreneur wants to learn about scaling, franchising and building a brand then Ray Kroc is certainly one of the pioneers of the fast food industry.

Persistence

Ray's story highlights few classic entrepreneur behaviours: Ray was a consummate salesman – he never gave up. He never took no for an answer, always exploring a solution, no matter how improbable it was to find one.

Persistence is an extremely important quality – it helps us accept feedback and overcome failure, and provides us the necessary pivot points in business.

Getting the process right

When Kroc secured the master franchising rights to McDonalds, he analysed every aspect of McDonald's operations. His idea of a franchise was one that could be reproduced again and again in cities and towns all over the country, would lead to the creation of the first fast food franchise mega chain.

He analysed every operational function of the original McDonald's from purchasing to prep to the inventory, cooking and cleaning. He strove for continuous refinements, and developed a comprehensive set of standards and procedures.

The ability to reinvent

Kroc had the innate ability to bounce back from failures and reinvent himself again. He had seen numerous failures across his professional life, but he was determined to succeed. His unwavering ability to reinvent himself, along with his confidence, was one of the key drivers of his entrepreneurial success.

Vision

Without supporting Ray's treatment of Richard and Maurice, it must be acknowledged that Ray had vision. He could see what the future of fast food industry would look like: modern, clean, efficient and timely. His focus on expansion gave the brand just the thrust it required, and catapulted it to another league.

Right people

After securing the franchising rights, Kroc suffered from business model and cash flow problems. Harry J. Sonneborn came to his rescue by advising him about a new business model, which is the most important financial decision in the company's history. Sonneborn advised Kroc to buy tracts of land to lease to franchisees who, as per the clauses of the franchise agreement, could only lease from Kroc. This ensured that Kroc received a steady, up-front revenue stream that began when an agreement started, and not months later, when the restaurant opened its door. His cash flow problems got resolved, which allowed land acquisition, which fuelled further expansion.

McDonald's present-day real estate holdings represent \$37.7Bn on its balance sheet, about 99% of the company's assets and about 35% of its global revenue2. Ray attributed the company's success greatly to Harry, who later went on to be the company's Chief Executive & President (but had a fallout with Ray later). This emphasizes the importance of hiring the right people.

Managing Cash Flow Efficiently

Several businesses keel over during the first one year, due to their operational inefficiencies, which may be due to ineffective cash flow, skyrocketing expenses. Ray realized the problem and fixed that first by bringing in Sorbonne. Once cash flow stability is achieved, every entrepreneur can focus on the path of growth.

Summary

Kroc was certainly not infallible. He was authoritative, pushy and demanding but at the same time, all his efforts in creating the first ever mega franchise team helped provide support and visibility to the concept of fast food.

Entrepreneurs and managers everywhere can learn from his persistence, his risk taking attitude, his bold vision and the ability to appoint the right people.

❑

11.
Richard Branson

Richard Branson is a English business tycoon who is known for his flamboyant showmanship as much for his adventure capitalism. He is also known for his over the top publicity stunts and eccentric business decisions. His maverick entrepreneurship style has made Virgin one of the most loved brands globally.

Today the Virgin empire spans more than 400 companies. Branson set up iconic brands such as Virgin Records, Virgin Atlantic, Virgin Galactic; was knighted in 2000 for his services to entrepreneurship. He was recognized as the Times 100 most influential people in the world in 2007.

Branson began his entrepreneurial career at the age of 16 in 1967 when he started a magazine called Student in the area of youth activism1. From there, he set up a mail-order business In 1970, subsequently opening a chain of record stores, Virgin Records. The 1980s saw a period of rapid expansion as Branson started Virgin Atlantic and expanded Virgin Records, subsequently starting many other companies.

He is known to have a never-say-die attitude and his indefatigable spirit has inspired countless entrepreneurs everywhere.

Early Years

Richard Branson was born in 1950 in Surrey to Edward and Eve Branson. Branson as a child he struggled with dyslexia,. However, he had the unconditional and unwavering support from his mother, Eve, who always encouraged him in his endeavours.

At the age of 16, he decided to drop out of school and establish a youth activism magazine, called Student. The first issue of Student was published in 1966. For that issue, Branson had secured $8,000 in advertising and published 50,000 copies.

After receiving both brickbats and acclaim for this first entrepreneurial venture, Branson continued down the path of entrepreneurship.

He started Virgin Records in 1972, in collaboration with Nik Powell and invested in a recording studio. Virgin Records started its journey by tying up with those artists which other studios were reluctant to sign, ultimately becoming the world's largest independent record label.

However, after its initial success, Virgin Records struggled financially and in 1992, the problems peaked. The company was struggling to just stay afloat. Branson had to eventually sell Virgin Records to EMI for $1 billion.

Continuously adding new companies in the Virgin portfolio, such as Virgin Holidays, Virgin Express, Virgin Rail Group, Virgin

Mobile, Branson finally launched a company in the area of space tourism in 2004, called Virgin Galactic. Other ventures include Virgin Comics, Virgin Animation, Virgin Money, Virgin Hotels, and Virgin Healthcare.

Branson remains an iconic entrepreneur for his unique style of entrepreneurship, continuously innovating to challenge established market leaders and expanding Virgin's capabilities and scope of operations.

Management Lessons learnt from Richard Branson

Adventure

If there is one word that captures Richard's unique spirit of entrepreneurship it is adventure. Richard espouses adventure and zest for life. Since its launch, Virgin has captivated attention and held the imagination of people at large. The brand itself stands for fun and adventure, much like its founder.

The personality and the language of the brand and the founder are inextricably linked. Virgin has almost always competed with established players and its unique marketing and promotional activities have catapulted it into the limelight.

Resilience

Branson's entrepreneurial journey is full of resilience. In the early nineties, Virgin Records was struggling. To ensure that the other businesses did not suffer, Branson sold off Virgin Records. At that time, Virgin Atlantic was embroiled in a bitter and vicious battle with British Airways and Branson knew that in the long term, the sale would help Virgin tide over the tumultuous times.

Many of his other ventures also failed such as Virgin Cola, Virgin Cosmetics, and Virgin Brides. However, none of these failures deterred him.

Despite all these failures, Branson's indefatigable spirit helped him pursue despite these turbulent times. It demonstrates Branson's unstoppable spirit. He has publicly shared the learnings from each failure, demonstrating that failure is only a stepping stone for future success.

Courage to do Something New

Branson has always taken big, bold bets in business. When he started Virgin Atlantic, Branson's colleagues thought it was a laughable idea. Competing in the airlines industry against behemoths like British Airways was extremely difficult in those days. But Branson was determined. He felt there was a major gap in this area as commercial airlines companies no longer served the needs of the customers and he was convinced that there existed space in the market for an offering that provided an economical and enjoyable flying experience.

The story of Virgin Atlantic started when Branson was stranded in Puerto Rico while on his way to the British Virgin Islands. It was then that he was struck with the idea of starting his own airlines. He called up Boeing to enquire if they had any second hand 747s available, and with just one plane, Virgin Atlantic was launched.

Virgin was the first to offer services like seatback and stand-up bars, prioritizing adventure and customer service. At that time, British Airways tried few underhanded methods to force Virgin out of business. Branson sued for libel and won almost $1 million in damages, which were distributed to the airline's employees. It was known as the "the BA Christmas bonus," further highlighting how deeply Branson valued his employees.

Entrepreneurs can learn a lot from Branson's notions about winning against all the odds while competing against an entrenched competitor. Virgin competed with a much smaller fleet, against much bigger and established competitors to gain market share and delight customers. They fought and won against BA and it was telling that Branson distributed the settlement to employees, further winning the hearts of all his employees.

Embracing Failures

Virgin has had number of missteps along the way. One of Virgin's biggest failures has been Virgin Cola.

Virgin Cola was launched in 1994, and was received very well in the UK in the first two years. Branson also launched the product in the US market, driving a tank through the Times Square, colliding and crushing a massive wall of Coke cans.

But Coke retaliated. Coke struck up negotiations with retailers, obscuring Virgin Cola's presence on retailer shelves. Virgin Cola could capture only 0.5% of the US market share, eventually production was halted in 2012.

Another failure was Virgin Cars. Branson later said that they thought they had identified a gap in the retail market and wanted to transform the way cars were being sold. However, he felt later, in hindsight, the potential disruption was more around the actual product itself, and not in the selling process. Branson said that they did not anticipate the sustainability impact before launching the venture and felt that the best opportunities were later in the development of electric cars and clean fuels.

But Branson has never let failures deter him. His constant never-say-die attitude coupled with the ability to learn from every failure can certainly be emulated by entrepreneurs.

Innovation

In 2004, Branson founded Virgin Galactic, which develops commercial spacecraft and aims to provide suborbital spaceflights to space tourists. This is aligned to Branson's vision for space exploration and enabling this experience for other individuals. This is a strong testament to Branson's continued commitment to innovation despite past failures. More than 700 customers have expressed interest since the launch of the initiative.

Branson has also invested in Hyperloop One, further highlighting his commitment towards technologies and businesses of the future.

Philanthropy

Branson is known for philanthropic work, starting his first charity when he was just 17 years old. In 2009, he founded the Carbon War Room, which seeks solutions for global warming and the looming energy crisis. He also contributes to educational charities working in African countries. Further, he has pledged $3 billion to address global warming.

He also launched Virgin Start up – an initiative which provided loans to entrepreneurs between the ages of 18 and 30 across the UK.

Entrepreneurs can definitely imbibe the social entrepreneurship and philanthropic outlook Branson has. Such initiatives help addressing issues at the grassroots level and help in removing social inequities.

Summary

Richard Branson's take on entrepreneurship is remarkably different from what typical business magnates advise to do – specialization. The Virgin Group has more than 200 companies in his portfolio, resembling Branson's quest for constant innovation and doing something new. He has provided a tremendous example for all young entrepreneurs to carve their own path and not be guided by naysayers. His indefatigable attitude and never say die spirit will inspire countless entrepreneurs to embrace and learn from their failures.

❑

12. Warren Buffet

By far, he is the most prolific and successful investor of all times. Also known as the "Oracle of Omaha," he has a track record of unprecedented success.

Warren Buffet is the Chairman and the CEO of Berkshire Hathaway, which owns controlling stakes in more than 60 companies, including companies like Geico, Duracell and Dairy Queen. It also has holdings in Coca-Cola, Apple, American Express, Bank of America, and US Bancorp, amongst others.

Each Class A share of Berkshire Hathaway costs upwards of $330,000 – the most expensive share price of any company in history1. The stock price of Berkshire Hathaway's Class A stock has increased by more than 2,800,000% since 1965, underlying Buffet's investment acumen.

Buffet has been hugely influenced by Benjamin Graham in his investment approach, and his focus on value investing has seen him generate an average annualised gain of 20.8% per year.

Buffet bought his first stock at the age of 11 and filed his taxes first at the age of 13 – showing signs of being a prodigal success right from an early age.

He is also known for his philanthropic work – and for launching the Giving Pledge, together with Bill Gates, which encourages billionaires to donate at least half of their wealth to charitable causes.

Early years

Warren Buffett was born on 30th August, 1930, to Howard and Leila Buffet2. Howard was a stockbroker who later became a Congressman. Buffet was the second oldest child and displayed tremendous aptitude for investment and business, right since an early age2. As astonishing it may sound, Buffet purchased his first stock when he was eleven years old. He purchased three shares of Cities Service Preferred at $38 per share. Soon after, the stock price declined to just $27 per share. Warren displayed tremendous fortitude and held onto the stock till it rebounded to $40. Subsequently, he did sell of the Cities stock, but not without regret, as it bounded up again to $200. This experience taught Buffet his first lesson in investing: Patience is a virtue.

He was constantly interested in investing and business and his appetite was further heightened when he read a book called *One Thousand Ways to Make $1000*.

By the time Buffett was 15, he had earned enough from his business ventures to buy his first property for around $12003. It was a 40-acre farm in Nebraska and Buffett hired a tenant farmer who worked the land for him and Buffet received a share of the profits.

Upon his graduation, his father was keen that Warren should enrol at the Wharton School. Buffet studied business there for 2 years, but eventually moved to the University of Nebraska3. Buffet wanted to attend Harvard, but his candidature was rejected. He then chose to enrol at Columbia Business School, to learn from Benjamin Graham, a prolific investor himself and the author of the book, *The Intelligent Investor*.

Buffet was hugely influenced by Graham, eventually earning an A+ in his class, the only student ever to get that grade. After graduating, he was looking for opportunities to work. Eventually, after some time, Graham offered him a job at his partnership and in 1954, he moved back to New York to work there.

In 1956, Buffett decided to move back to Omaha to start his own partnership called Buffett Associates Ltd. With an investment from seven family members and friends of a total sum of $105,000 in total, the partnership commenced. Buffet had himself invested only $100. Given his acumen, the partnership flourished, and by the end of the year, he was managing around $300,000. He saw stupendous growth and his fame as an investor grew. In 1962, he began buying stock in a textile company called Berkshire Hathaway, eventually buying enough to gain controlling share and replaced the management. Berkshire Hathaway then went ahead to get ownership in many companies, including a 7% in Coca-Cola at that time.

Since then, Buffet's investment portfolio grew, adding more controlling stakes in companies and generating fabulous returns for investors.

In the late nineties, there was a boom of dot com companies and valuations of companies just launched totally defied stock market behaviour. Buffet did not participate in the heated valuations of tech companies, choosing to comply with the principles of value investing. In hindsight, he was proved right. The dot com bubble burst and the stock market reverted to recognizing intrinsic value and his long term approach again gained credence.

Management Lessons Kearnt from Warren Buffet

Business Acumen

Buffet was always interested in maximizing his investments and pursued entrepreneurial ventures even when he was in school. In high school, he and his friend bought a pinball machine and displayed it in a barbershop. With the money they earned off the pinball machine, they bought more machines and eventually had a total of eight of them.

Buffett proceeded to buy stocks and started his own business after graduating from Columbia. By the time he was 26, Buffet's personal wealth was $174,000, equivalent to about $1.4 million today.

If there is one thing that entrepreneurs can learn from Buffet, it is that starting investing when you are young is advantageous.

Frugality

The next lesson that everyone can learn from Warren Buffet is frugality. Despite being one of the wealthiest persons across the globe, he has a very simple lifestyle. He lives in the same house he bought back in the 1950s. Buffet has always advocated the power of savings and living simply, going against the grain of modern day consumerism.

He is known to abhor excesses, and has criticized executive compensation at the cost of shareholder losses, rebuking those companies that do not penalize executives for faulty decision making that ultimately does not impact them but rather shareholders.

Decision Making

Buffet is renowned for his astute decision making skills. Rather than speed in decision making, Buffet is known for his informed decision making, favouring research over emotion.

He recalls some decisions such as his acquisition of Tesco in which Berkshire Hathaway owned 415 million shares in 2012. In 2014, the company overstated its profits and stock prices tumbled. In his letter to shareholders in 2014, Buffet mentioned that he had concerns about Tesco's management, which led to his decision for the sale of his stock, resulting in a $43 million profit. However, he felt he didn't move fast enough. The move cost the company a $444 million after-tax loss.

He has highlighted the losses of not following up on research based decision making enough. Entrepreneurs should definitely take a leaf out of his book and sharpen their evidence-based decision making skills.

Knowing When to Quit

Another skill that entrepreneurs can definitely learn from Warren is knowing when to quit.

Buffet has acknowledged that despite being a prolific investor, he also makes mistakes. But he quickly amends his mistakes and doesn't repeat them.

In the mid-nineties, Buffet bought a company called Dexter Shoe for around $400 million. But the purchase went south – Buffet later reflected that that $400 million worth of Berkshire stock which he used to make the acquisition would have been $400 billion.

In his annual letter to shareholders in 2007, Buffett admitted that the decision cost the investors $3.5 billion. At the time, this was 1.6 percent of Berkshire Hathaway's net worth.

It is important to know when to quit in a losing situation. He is known to have remarked that "Should you find yourself in a chronically leaking boat, energy devoted to changing vessels is likely to be more productive than energy devoted to patching leaks."

Entrepreneurs can be very passionately involved with their business idea. But they should know when to walk away from a loss. Given the market dynamics, better quality businesses always flourish and compound cash flows, eroding low to medium quality products in the long run.

Embracing Failures

Buffet has always acknowledged his failures publicly. In his 2013 letter to shareholders, he explained his rationale behind the purchase of Energy Future Holdings.

Berkshire Hathaway had acquired Energy Future bonds worth $2 billion. Buffet's rationale was that utilities tend to perform well even in recessions, and can generate earnings from a variety of sources that reduce the power of any single regulator.

However, trouble began brewing at Energy Futures and he had an inkling that it would file for bankruptcy. In 2013, Berkshire eventually sold the holding for $259 million but suffered an $873 million pre-tax loss.

Similarly, Berkshire had invested in a company in 2016 called Precision Castparts as a long term bet on the civil aerospace sector, buying the firm for $32 billion6. However, the company shed more than 40% of its workforce, in 2020. Berkshire had to write off around $9.8 billion on Precision's value last year, due to demand contraction due to COVID.

Philanthropy

Buffett has championed the cause of taxation of the rich and has pledged to donate 99% of his fortune to philanthropic causes, mainly via the Gates Foundation. In 2009, He co-founded The Giving Pledge in 2009 with Bill Gates, pledging to donate his wealth through charity.

Summary

Warren Buffet has remained an iconic investor and a huge source of inspiration for entrepreneurs everywhere. Entrepreneurs should also draw inspiration from his philanthropic work.

❑

13.
Howard Schultz

Introduction

Who hasn't heard of Starbucks?

Howard Schultz, Chairman of Starbucks, turned this regional coffee company into one of the most iconic brands globally.

Starbucks is not just a coffee place, it has evolved into a multi-cultural institution, where social experiences come alive. Starbucks has been credited with reviving the coffee culture in the US. As in 2020, the company had more than 30,000 stores in 83 countries, making it an important social hub for people across the globe.

Schultz joined the company in 1982, left in 1985, launching his own venture which eventually acquired Starbucks in 1987. He served as Chairman and CEO from 1987 to 20001, helming the company again from 2008 to 2018. In 2018, Schultz stepped down as executive chairman and board member of the company and became chairman emeritus.

Early years

Schultz was born in 1953, in Brooklyn, New York, to Fred and Elaine Schultz, and grew up in federally subsidized housing in Canarsie, which exposed him to the exposed him to the world's wealth disparity early on in life.

He was very interested in sports and found that sports could be a route to education and a better life. He enrolled in Northern Michigan University in 1971 with the hope of getting a football scholarship, but it never materialized. He undertook student loans and did part time jobs to finance his education, graduating in 1975.

He started his career with Xerox, in the sales training program, eventually becoming a salesman. In 1979, he moved to a Swedish company, Perstorp, which was planning to set up a US division for its Hammarplast housewares subsidiary. He was transferred to New York after being promoted as Vice President of Hammarplast.

In 1981, while working at Hammarplast, he noticed that a retailer in Seattle was placing an usually large number of orders for drip coffee machines. Intrigued by the number of orders, Schultz then travelled to Seattle to meet the Starbucks team – the company's then owners, Gerald Baldwin and Gordon Bowker.

He was amazed at the passion of the founders for coffee and the retail operation staff's skill and expertise of the brew. Even though at that time it appealed to only a small niche of gourmet coffee enthusiasts, Schultz could see the potential of coffee.

A year later, Schultz came on board as the director of retail operations and marketing. At the time, Starbucks only had 3 stores.

In 1983, Schutz was on a business trip to Milan, where he walked into an Italian café and tasted his first espresso. He was captivated by the beverage, the experience of the café atmosphere. Starbucks stores at that time only sold whole bean coffee and had no seating. Howard had a vision of creating specialty coffee stores that integrated the coffee drinking experience and strengthened community bonding. The founders of Starbucks, however, weren't interested in his idea.

In 1985, Schultz left Starbucks to pursue his idea of launching an Italian-like experience for coffee-lovers. His company was named Il Giornale (Italian for "the daily"). He had to secure nearly $1.6 million in funding for Il Giornale, Howard raised the funds from local investors. Il Giornale opened its first store in 1986. By 1987, Il Giornale had three expresso bars.

In the same year, 1987, the original founders of Starbucks were looking to sell the company. In 1981, one of the founders, Gordon Bowker, had opened a second beverage business, Red Hook Brewery, and decided to redirect his energy and efforts fully on Red Hook. Schultz was offered a 90-day exclusive to raise the funds.

In August 1987, Il Giornale acquired Starbucks for $3.8 million, and Schultz became CEO of Starbucks Corporation. At the time, there were six stores.

In 1992, Starbucks listed public on the NASDAQ through an IPO, its revenues that year were $93 million from 165 stores.

Since then, it has grown, achieving one milestone after another, opening its first store outside North America in 1996 (in Japan & Singapore), acquiring Tazo Tea in 1999, opening stores in China, South Korea, Kuwait, and Lebanon, having around 15,000 stores in 20071. In 2008, Schultz returned as CEO to begin a transformation of the company, after years of declining sales and departure from core values.

Management Lessons Learnt from Howard Schultz

Vision

Schultz is known to be a visionary individual. He could foresee the potential of the coffee experience right in the 1980s, when the concept of coffee bars was still nascent and not as all pervasive as it is today. He was bold enough to leave his job at Starbucks to pursue his dream of what he believed was a sustainable and profitable business idea to launch his own venture, Il Giornale, eventually acquiring Starbucks.

Young entrepreneurs should certainly learn how to identify high potential opportunities and invest early on to create a unique business advantage.

Employees First

If there is one thing that characterizes Schultz's management philosophy, it is his attitude towards his employees. When Schultz was young, he noticed that his father was rendered helpless upon being injured in the course of his work. Without healthcare and any assistance, young Schultz's family suffered.

That experience stayed with Schultz who vowed to create an enterprise that would provide for its employees in times of need. In 1988, Starbucks became one of the first retail organizations to offer healthcare to every employee, including contractual workers, as well as stock options.

Schultz's attitude towards his employees is evident in the way he addresses them, choosing to call them partners. Throughout his tenure at Starbucks, Schultz has always prioritized his employees and their well-being. In a collaboration with Arizona State University, the company announced it would pay employees' full four-year college tuition for their online degree program, further investing in their education and growth.

Starbucks had also announced that it would hire 10,000 military veterans and their spouses by 2018. To help launch the careers of the underprivileged youth, the company promised to hire 10,000 16 to 24 year-olds, further helping marginalized sections of the society to seek employment.

In 1991, Starbucks started offering company stock, affectionately referred to as "Bean Stock," to employees, making them partners in the company.

Schultz empathetic and employee first policies are certainly worth emulating by all young entrepreneurs.

Ethical Management

In April 2019, two black customers were arrested when they were waiting to order in the store, by a 911 call dialled by the Philadelphia Starbucks manager6. The men were waiting for a meeting to kick-off and were surprised by the attitude of the store manager. Needless to say, Starbucks was widely criticized for this racially biased move. The company later closed all the stores on May 29 for a racial bias education program. On the program, CBS "60 Minutes", Schultz disclosed that "We had a moral obligation as a company to discuss this."

Schultz's public ownership of the company's shortcomings and the desire to correct them has always helmed the company away from most crises.

Under Schultz's leadership, the company also made ethical sourcing of coffee bean a priority. In 1999, the company partnered with Conservation International to promote sustainable coffee-growing practices1. In 2000, it established licensing agreement with TransFair USA to sell Fairtrade certified coffee in U.S. and Canada. Finally, in 2001 it introduced ethical coffee-sourcing guidelines developed in partnership with Conservation International. In 2015, Starbucks reached the 99% ethically sourced coffee milestone.

The company is also conscious of its carbon footprint, launching the industry's first paper beverage cup containing post-consumer recycled fiber in 2006.

Innovation

Schultz has always embraced innovation. Right from the launch of the concept coffee café's to product and service innovation, Starbucks has been a hub of ideas. Some of the innovations launched at Starbucks include the idea submission platform: MyStarbucksIdeas.com; introduction of instant coffee, VIA; introduction of custom-designed espresso machine: Mastrena; creation of a signature blend, Pike Place Roast; reinvigorating the Loyalty Program.

Even in retail operations, it is possible to continuously launch new and innovative ways of meeting customer's expectations.

Focus on Core Values

Starbucks went through an existential and leadership crisis in 2000s. One reason that has been cited as key to Starbucks' downfall was the pursuit of relentless growth. During that decade, opening new stores across the world became the number 1 focus of the company. The company also ventured into businesses such as entertainment and started stocking and selling unrelated merchandise at its stores.

All of this adversely impacted customer satisfaction, brand image, partner engagement.

In the midst of the 2008 recession, Schultz took a painful decision to close many stores and laying off employees to save Starbucks.

He is said to have cited "Success is not sustainable if it's defined by how big you become. Large numbers that once captivated me—40,000 stores—are not what matters. The only number that matters is 'one'. One cup. One customer. One partner. One experience at a time. We had to get back to what mattered most."

Crisis Management

Schultz is always recognized to be empathetic and transparent. Upon returning to helm Starbucks in 2008, he noticed that the company was in crisis. The brand's once likeable and iconic image had suffered due to incessantly trying to compete with Dunkin' Donuts and McDonald's, stocking breakfast sandwiches and sacrificing atmosphere along the way. Obviously, there was a huge impact on stocks as well, with the stock price decreasing by 42% in 2007.

Schultz knew that this problem would be solved by being radically transparent and open. He tendered an open apology to his employees, and shared the truth during an meeting with nearly 12,000 Starbucks store managers.

The company leadership at that time thought that being open and transparent would be detrimental to the present state of the company, but Howard was insistent on managing the crisis with transparency.

He is said to have remarked "How could I ask something of them if they didn't have the total picture, the total understanding of what the situation was and how dire it was? I knew instinctively that I needed to share with them 100% of the truth."

Summary

Entrepreneurs can learn a very important lesson in transparency from Schultz. In an era of unethical business practices and corrupt, self-serving leadership, Howard Schultz has shown that it is possible to lead with honesty, transparency and empathy. Difficulties during his early years did not discourage Schultz from pursuing his entrepreneurial dreams, and his tenacity helped him create an iconic customer brand globally, inspiring millions of entrepreneurs.

❑

14. Andrew Carnegie

Introduction

Andrew Carnegie is not recognized today because of the massive steel empire that he founded and presided over but for his magnanimous and benevolent philanthropy which helped fund institutions, libraries, and other educational projects across arts, science, technology and culture which have benefited millions across the globe.

Carnegie's parents emigrated to the United States when he was 12. His grit and determination to build a better life for himself and his family led him on a journey where he constantly learnt and upskilled himself, took risks and launched his own venture, ultimately building an empire which was valued at $350 million (worth about $4.8 billion today) at its peak.

He had business interests in railroads, railroad sleeping cars, oil derricks and bridges. He ultimately sold his flagship company, the Carnegie Steel Company, to J. P. Morgan in 1901 for $480 million and surpassed J. D. Rockefeller as the wealthiest man in America for a few years.

Carnegie gave away the majority of his wealth away as charity and endowments. He passed away died at age 83 having created a legacy that has lasted centuries.

Early years

Carnegie was born in Scotland to a weaving family, to Will and Margaret, in the town of Dunfermline, Scotland's historic medieval capital. Due to the rise of industrialism, home weaving became obsolete and his family fell upon hard times. His parents emigrated to America in 1848 along with his younger brother, Tom.

They landed in New York and subsequently made their way to Allegheny, Pennsylvania, a place where they had relatives1.

Carnegie started working young, at the age of 13, earning $1.20 in a week, carrying bobbins to loom workers in a Pittsburgh cotton factory. Subsequently, he began working as a messenger in the local telegraph company, and was promoted as a telegraph operator. His breakthrough came when he secured a job at the Pennsylvania Railroad, where he promoted to the role of a superintendent at the age of 24.

He continuously kept on reading and educating himself, looking for opportunities where he could learn something new.

Carnegie's boss at the Pennsylvania Railroad, Thomas A. Scott, apprised him that the Adams Express Company intended to sell 10 shares3. Carnegie seized this opportunity and raised the capital by mortgaging his parents' house to get $5003. Once the dividends started coming in, he expanded his investments to iron, coal, and oil companies.

Railroads were the new oil at that time, and a source of constant innovation and consequently wealth. Carnegie was then approached by Theodore Woodruff who pitched the idea of sleeping cars on railways. He also offered Carnegie a share in the Woodruff Sleeping Car Company. Carnegie accepted Woodruff's proposal and secured a bank loan.

Carnegie left the railroad company in 1865, continuously learning, observing and investigating ways how to expand his investments. He founded ventures such as an iron bridge building company, steamers, railroads, oil wells and a telegraph company, amassing a fortune by the time he was in his early 30s. He subsequently set up a steel production plant and Carnegie Steel Corporation became the largest steel manufacturing company in the world.

He fortified his steel empire reducing factory inefficiencies and optimizing raw materials, and transportation infrastructure, subsequently merging his primary holdings in 1892 to the Carnegie Steel Company.

He sold his steel business to another business magnate, banker J. P. Morgan in 1901 for $480 million. Finally, Morgan merged Carnegie Steel with other steel companies to form the largest steel conglomerate, US Steel.

After the sale of his steel business, Carnegie retired from business and pursued philanthropy full time, authoring his iconic work in 1889, titled "The Gospel of Wealth".

Management Lessons Learnt from Andrew Carnegie

Welfare Capitalism

Carnegie believed in the concept of welfare capitalism. He strongly believed that the wealthier section of the society should shun excesses and use their wealth to provide for the upliftment of society. He also authored a book titled The Gospel of Wealth, which articulated his views on wealth distribution and capitalism.

Carnegie felt that the best way of dealing with wealth inequity was to utilize it in way that benefited the society. He was vehemently against wasteful expenditures of the rich and abhorred traditional bequests, wealth handed down from generation to generation, and wealth willed to the state for public purposes6. Carnegie also advocated against extravagant spending, irresponsible spending or self-indulgence and felt it was the responsibility of the wealthy to take steps to reduce the inequities between the rich and poor.

Understanding People

Carnegie is known to have remarked that understanding people was his core strength in building a huge business empire.

"I did not understand steam machinery, but I tried to understand that much more complicated piece of mechanism—man."

Carnegie launched many ventures, from railroads to a steel company. He leveraged his understanding of people as fundamental drivers for the business. By hiring the right talent for the right roles, he was able to scale his businesses to eventually build a massive empire1. Entrepreneurs can learn that how important it is to recruit and nurture the right talent in their ventures early on.

Focus

Carnegie was a huge believer in focus. He believed that the road to success in any field demanded mastery in that. He advised against scattering one's resources in too many directions and felt that an individual specializing in one area was bound to become an expert in that area.

He is said to have remarked7:

"My advice to young men would be not only to concentrate

their whole time and attention on the one business in life in which they engage, but to put every dollar of their capital into it."

Entrepreneurs can certainly learn from Carnegie's advice and strategize on how to attain specialization and expertise. Focus leads to single minded pursuit of one's desired area of excellence and certainly leads to growth and development.

Exercising Initiative

Carnegie came from a disadvantaged background, but he never let that stand in his way of improvement. He constantly read and educated himself and took. Initiatives and challenges at work to ultimately start his own venture1. Remarking upon his rise from a telegraph messenger boy to a telegraph operator, he said that finding the operating rooms available in the morning, he chanced upon an opportunity to practice the telegraph instruments before the operators arrived and commenced their work. He gradually began receiving the responsibility of watching the instruments when the operators took a break, ultimately learning the art of telegraphy. When a position opened up, at the age of 16, Carnegie was chosen to fill it. He then rose to the position of a personal telegraph operator for Thomas A. Scott, the superintendent of the western division of the Pennsylvania Railroad Company1,3. He again took initiatives in his new job, once giving orders to the trains for clearing up a backlog arising due to an accident, again proving his mettle as an able decision maker. Because of his initiative taking ability, Carnegie was appointed as the superintendent of the railroad's Pittsburgh Division.

Managers and entrepreneurs can definitely achieve a lot by taking initiative whenever possible. Taking initiative can also help us learn new skills and discover previously unknown strengths.

Business Acumen

Carnegie had developed a remarkably sharp business acumen – anticipating growth areas before they became mainstream. In

1864, he became one of the early investors in an oil company – the Columbia Oil Company in Pennsylvania. This investment yielded over $1,000,000 in cash dividends in one year, and petroleum from oil wells on the property sold profitably. The demand for iron products during wartime such as armour, shells, cannons, and other industrial products skyrocketed. Carnegie established number of companies in this area, such as a steel rolling mill, steel production and profited from the increased demand.

Post the war, Carnegie exited the railroads business and focused on the ironworks trade, eventually forming the Keystone Bridge Works and the Union Ironworks, in Pittsburgh.

Innovation

Carnegie built up the most extensive integrated iron and steel manufacturing set up He leveraged two key innovations during his time, the first of which was the adoption of Bessemer process, which led to the high carbon content of pig iron to be burnt away in an accelerated but controlled technique during steel production. The prices of the final output dropped and the process was widely adopted for rails.

Carnegie also oversaw the largest vertical integration of all suppliers of raw materials. Carnegie had control over the manufacture of largest manufacturer of pig iron, steel rails, and coke in the world in 1880s, with a production capacity of approximately 2,000 tons of pig iron per day1. In 1883, Carnegie acquired the manufacturing set up of Homestead Steel Works, a close rival, which included an extensive plant served by tributary coal and iron fields, a 700 km long railway, and a line of lake steamships, further augmenting his empire. He finally consolidated all his assets in 1892 with the formation of the Carnegie Steel Company.

Philanthropy

Carnegie gave away approximately $350 million, which would be in billions today, almost entirely the bulk of his wealth, to charity. His endowments helped fund the establishment of more than 2,500 public libraries around the world and helped set up eminent institutions in area of arts, science, education, amongst other areas. His endowment help the construction of the legendary concert venue in New York in 1982, named after him, Carnegie Hall. Other institutions that came to life because of him were The Carnegie Mellon University, The Carnegie Institution for Science, and the Carnegie Foundation.

Carnegie is often referred to as the "Patron Saint of Libraries" as he spent nearly $55 million of his wealth on libraries alone. He believed libraries were an important part of self-education of anyone in America, and also helped immigrants with the knowledge needed for cultural assimilation.

Apart from libraries and universities, he established several trusts such as Carnegie Museums of Pittsburgh, Carnegie Institution for Science, the Carnegie Trust for the Universities of Scotland, Carnegie Foundation, Carnegie Dunfermline Trust, Carnegie Foundation for the Advancement of Teaching, Carnegie Endowment for International Peace, and the Carnegie UK Trust.

Summary

Andrew Carnegie is a doyen of philanthropy and welfare in the times of relentless capitalism. He has inspired countless generations to come with his selfless endowments and helped further the cause of art, science, and culture.

❑

15. Henry Ford

Modern industrialization owes a great deal to Henry Ford, the man who is credited with bringing the assembly line manufacturing method to factory production.

Ford was the founder of the Ford Motor Company, an accomplished industrialist and business magnate. By creating the first affordable automobile, he converted the automobile from an luxury into a necessity for Americans, a strategy that immensely impacted the lifestyle of 20th century.

His introduction of the Model T automobile transformed the automobile industry radically. It introduced economies of scale, production efficiency, standardization and unleashed the power of American capitalist development in the world.

Though Ford was not an inventor; he did not invent the automobile or the assembly line production technique, but he is credited with the introduction of modern manufacturing methods that made mass production possible, leading to economies of scale and reducing the price points of goods. His contribution to industrial development, right from mass market production, introduction of higher wages for workers, the introduction of the 5-day work week, all are in use even today.

Born on July 30, 1863 in Michigan, Ford's parents were William Ford and Mary Ford. Ford's interest in machinery developed from a young age, when in 1879, Ford worked as an apprentice machinist in Detroit, with James F. Flower and Bros., and later with the Detroit Dry Dock Company. In 1882, upon his return to Dearborn, he became proficient at operating the Westinghouse portable steam engine. He was later hired by Westinghouse to service their steam engines, further increasing his exposure and interest in mechanical equipment.

In 1885, Ford repaired an Otto engine and five years later, in 1890, Ford commenced work on a two-cylinder engine. In 1892, he finished assembling his first motor car, replete with a two-cylinder four horsepower motor.

The vehicle that Ford developed, travelled about 1000 miles between 1895 and 1896, Encouraged by this, Ford then started work on a second car in 1896, eventually building three cars in his home workshop.

A little known fact is Ford's association with Edison; Ford became an engineer with at Edison in 1891. After his promotion to Chief Engineer in 1893, he was able to further his experiments on gasoline engines. This ultimately led to the development of the Ford Quadricycle, a self-propelled vehicle.

However, Ford's most iconic contribution to the automobile industry, and more to transportation, The Model T, debuted on October 1, 1908. It pioneered some changes that exist till date. The incorporation of the steering wheel on the left was immediately copied by other companies. The car was easy to drive and maintain, enabling large swathes of the American population to drive.

In 1913, Ford introduced the concept of assembly line production, which fuelled a massive production increase. Though Ford popularized the idea, it is thought that it was suggested by employees. Meanwhile, the success of model T earned some competition, and by the mid-1920s, General Motors had become a serious contender for Ford. GM adopted a price laddering strategy, which enabled the company to cater to different audience segments, unlike Ford's focus on the mass market segment. The market was further transformed with the introduction of ideas like payment plans for cars.

Eventually, the sales of Model T plateaued off, and Ford was forced to commence work on a revised model, shutting down production for 18 months. At around the same time, Ford constructed a massive new assembly plant at River Rouge for the new Model A, which launched in 1927.

Ford championed innovation and welfare capitalism at the same time, pioneering many industry-firsts, such as initiatives to improve the condition of workers and to reduce turnover. In1926, he announced the five day workweek, prior to this he had set the benchmark by increasing the wages of his factory employees, thus building on his idea of welfare capitalism.

Management Lessons Learnt from Ford

So what are the management lessons one can hope to learn from Ford?

Market Knowledge

Ford is said to have remarked "If I had simply asked people what they wanted, they would have asked me for faster horses!"

Like most visionary innovators, Ford knew and anticipated the customer needs before they even knew it existed. He was able to weld his deep interest in automobiles with his passion of democratizing automobile ownership, thus impacting the lifestyle of a generation of Americans, and eventually, everywhere around the world.

Though he did not invent the automobile, but his experiments with assembling one, plus his interests in machines, offered him the requisite knowledge to know which product was right for the market.

By the time the Model T was introduced, Ford already had his pulse on the market, knowing which product was right for the target market.

Driving Efficiencies

Ford was a master of efficiency. Right from developing the assembly line style of production, resulting in massive economies of scale, to optimizing production workflows. He invested in increasing worker wages, stabilizing the workforce attrition, again leading to efficiency.

Even though common sense went against it, but Ford's apparently generous decision to increase wages of workers, nearly doubling it, was driven by a desire for efficiency. Model T's production figures were rising—in a factory which was running on conveyor belts. This modern transportation system within the factory transported small parts to workers, each of whom were tasked with performing a specific action. The need for highly skilled workforce decreased, and the need for workers who could competently perform monotonous, repetitive tasks well increased. To combat the issue of chronic absenteeism and staff turnover, Ford offered higher wages, in the hope it would stabilize the workforce and attract a more reliable workforce, and it did.

Without any additional investments in workforce, the assembly line introduction helped in skyrocketing production. This allowed him to make Model T even more competitively priced, without hurting the company's bottom line.

Laser Focus

Other competitors began offering automobiles for every price segment, but Ford was clear about the segment that he would create products for. He wanted automobiles to become accessible by everyone. All his experiments in efficiency were designed with the single focus of providing better automobiles to his target segment, at a cost lower than before.

Employee Engagement

Ford's policies on workforce compensation, culture, and production are all forebearers of modern day workplaces. Many of his contributions are followed to date.

Ford's experiments in wage increase also is a case study in talent acquisition. In 1914, Ford was one of the first organizations to offer a $5 per day wage, which was more than double of the prevalent wage rate for that time. He also extended his highest performers a higher wage rate. He also introduced the 40 hour work week, providing employees the weekend off. Many of these practices continue to be followed in modern manufacturing till date. These practices reduced employee turnover, but more importantly, attracted the brightest and best talent to come work at Ford. These employees brought with them their expertise and experience, raising productivity, and lowered employee training costs.

Summary

On many counts, Ford is considered to be a visionary, with ideas and innovation ahead of his time. The magnitude of his contributions can be gauged by the impact it has had on modern transportation and democratizing the use of the automobile.

His actions have continued to inspire and will further inspire a generation of entrepreneurs.

❑

16.
JRD Tata

Introduction

Jehangir Ratanji Dadabhoy (JRD) Tata was an Indian entrepreneur, avid aviator, and chairman of the Tata Group. Also known as the father of Indian civil aviation, Tata was the founder of the first commercial airline in India, known as Tata Airlines in 1932.

JRD remains a colossal figure in the India business ecosystem, as he was known for his ethical conduct of business, philanthropy, worker welfare schemes as well as support of national projects in science, research, arts and education.

Under his helm, the total assets of the Tata Group grew from

US$100 million to over US$5 billion. The total number of group companies also expanded from 14 to 95.

JRD Tata was not just a doyen of the Indian business ecosystem but a compassionate industrialist. His contribution to expanding business, economic growth, social capitalism and science and research is unparalleled. He will remain an inspiration for countless entrepreneurs for years to come.

Early years

Born on 29th July in 1904 in Paris, JRD Tata was the son of Ratanji Dadabhoy Tata and Suzanne Brière. He was educated in France, Japan and UK. He also served in the French army for a period of one year.

He lost his mother when he was 19, and his father, at the age of 22. In 1938, JRD was unanimously elected and appointed as the Chairman of the Tata Group in a special board meeting. Though he was just 33 at that time, he had made tremendous strides in business by then through the creation of Associated Cement Company (ACC), Tata Airlines and numerous other business advancements.

He took over from Sir Nowroji Saklatvala and was the youngest member of the Tata Sons board. Under his leadership, the group expanded its scope of services from chemicals, tea, automobiles, and information technology.

The years following his appointment were the ones in which the Tata Group expanded its footprint: In 1939, Tata Chemicals was launched, followed by TELCO In 1945, and Air India in 1948.

JRD was keen that the businesses be run by management professionals, and he transformed the Tata Group into a business conglomerate where talent was nurtured and groomed.

JRD passed away in 1993 in Geneva, Switzerland from a kidney infection5. Upon his death, the Indian Parliament was adjourned in his memory. His monumental contribution to Indian business and the Tata Group will continue to inspire people for decades to come.

Management Lessons Learnt from JRD Tata

Innovation

JRD was an avid aviator1. He launched Tata Airlines at a time when the aviation industry was still nascent and there was a tremendous interest in aviation and technology, after the World Wars. He was India's first licensed pilot and is known at the Father of the Indian Aviation industry1. JRD anticipated the opportunity of civil aviation, and launched Tata Airlines from a point of his personal interest in aviation.

Diversification

Under JRD's leadership, the Tata Group entered new businesses, many of them novel and with immense future potential.

The Tatas invested in core industries through companies like Tata Steel and Tata Chemicals, which was aligned to JRD's vision of building India's industrial strength through development of core industries2. Many of these companies were capital intensive, and open to interventions from the government. But the Tata Group persevered in their commitment to building the economic muscle of the nation.

Right from hotels to airlines, trucks, soda ash, and air conditioning and financial services, the Tata Group became a behemoth under his guidance. He strengthened each business, consolidating those which were necessary.

In 1936, eleven cement companies belonging to prominent industrialists, including the Tatas, F E Dinshaw, Khataus, and Nixon groups were merged to form a single company known as The Associated Cement Companies. It was the first notable merger in the country6. This consolidation helped these companies to face and fight the competition in a small aggressive market. The move helped establish the country's nascent cement industry and signalled a time of mutual cooperation.

Tata Chemicals was launched in 1939, with the vision that it could pioneer the inorganic chemical industry for India. India's future manufacturing strength in the area of ceramics, textiles, glass and other industries depended on India's self-reliance on soda ash. Tata Chemicals was a brave step in building this self-reliance.

Tata Finlay was a JV with the James Finlay Company in the area of manufacturing packed tea for the domestic market and instant tea for exports. In 1983, James Finlay looked for liquidation of the partnership, Tata Tea was formed, further strengthening Tata's footprint in the consumer industry.

Innovation

JRD had a personal interest in technology. JRD felt that the Tata Group was rightly placed to establish a world class engineering organization. Tata Steel felt like the perfect springboard for his vision. A Research and Control Laboratory had been established in Tata Steel in 1937, and the team developed a wide variety of special steels for commercial applications. Tata Locomotive and Engineering Company (TELCO) was incorporated as a public limited company in September 1945 and very soon it received a certificate to commence production of boilers and locomotives8. It also began planning a foray into heavy engineering equipment, such as earthmoving equipment, diesel engines, road rollers and so on.

The Tata Consultancy Services (TCS) was launched in 1968, and grew in both number of people employed, and profitability. JRD was a visionary who anticipated future changes and helped fortify the Tata Group and cemented its place further in the echelons of business advancements.

Training

JRD was extremely invested in talent development in the Tata Group. For training and upskilling of employees, he established the Tata Administrative Service and the Tata Management Training Centre at Pune.

TAS is the leadership development program for young talent across the 100+ group companies. It was initiated by JRD in 1956, to create a strong pipeline of leadership talent that could be tapped across the Tata group of companies.

Humanitarian Schemes

Under JRD's leadership, a number of employee welfare schemes were introduced in the Tata Group. These employee reforms were introduced much before compliance was mandated by law – emphasizing the compassionate industrialism practiced by JRD. Leave with pay was introduced in Tata Steel in 1920, it was established by law only in 1945. Tata Steel set up a provident fund way back in 1920, but it received legal approval only in 1952. Also introduced were gratuities, medical services, maternity benefits, accident insurance schemes and the eight-hour shift.

The government imbibed some of his reforms, and introduced the Employees' State Insurance Scheme of India, the Factories Act, 1948 and the Employees Provident Funds and Miscellaneous Provisions Act, 1952, underscoring JRD's contribution in this area.

Contribution to Research

JRD's contribution to setting up eminent institutions in the area of science and research is immeasurable. He helped set up The Tata Institute of Fundamental Research, the Tata Memorial Hospital, the Tata Institute of Social Sciences, the National Institute of Advanced Sciences and the National Centre for the Performing Arts .

All these institutions helped strengthen India's science and R&D capital.

Managing Crisis

During his tenure at the helm of the Tata Group, JRD had weathered many a crisis. But none was so wide ranging in its impact as one in 1970. After the Prime Minister Indira Gandhi led government came to power in 1966, a legislation was introduced to limit the scope and scale of private companies. This legislation led to the abolition of the managing agency system, and under the new system, each Tata company became an independent entity with its own board of directors.

This legislation impacted The Tata Group, as the influence of the Tata Sons was no longer implementable, and its role became limited to advise and persuasion. At that time, up to 74% of the group was run by managing agencies, to comply with the new legislation, the Group had to identify and appoint hundreds of independent directors for all its companies2. The exercise was carried out by the eminent jurist, Nani Palkhivala, who became a part of Tata Sons as a director in 1961 and remained J.R.D.'s legal counsel for the next many decades. J.R.D. nominated the managing director in each company and another director from the Tata ecosystem. Directors were also appointment from outside the group, giving the companies sufficient autonomy. Industry peers commended his statesman-like handling of this crisis.

Philanthropy

JRD was an immensely compassionate person – business and philanthropy were closely related for him.

His industry peers were known for lavish personal expenditures. JRD invested the profits back into the group companies and make philanthropic contributions for nation building. Right from building institutions of national eminence, to support causes for upliftment of the worthy but disadvantaged, JRD did not shy away from investing his personal wealth for just causes. In 1944, he set up the JRD Tata Trust. Subsequently, he sold some more of his shares and an apartment that he owned in Mumbai to establish the JRD and Thelma Tata Trust, which works in the area of helping disadvantaged women.

Summary

JRD was a doyen that continues to inspire countless entrepreneurs even today. His compassion, commitment and vision helped fortify the Tata Group and the nation at the same time.

❑

17.
Mukesh Ambani

Introduction

There is no way that a mention of the Indian business ecosystem does not mention the contribution and the presence of the Ambanis. Founded by the legendary tycoon Dhirubhai Ambani, Reliance Industries has gone on to achieve immense stature and respect, and is a hallmark of ambitious growth.

Taking the helm from his father, Mukesh Ambani, charted a new era of growth in Reliance.

Mukesh is now the chairman and managing director of Reliance Industries Limited (RIL) and has been on the board of

Reliance since 1977. A chemical engineer and MBA by education , Mukesh has ushered a new era in Reliance. He also has ownership in the Indian Premier League franchise Mumbai Indians through Reliance.

Mukesh kickstarted Reliance's backward integration journey – ensuring Reliance owned the full value chain, right from upstream businesses such as oil and gas exploration and production of petrochemicals and petroleum refining to polyester fibres and textiles down the value chain.

His residence, the Antilia is one of the most expensive private residences in the world, being valued at $1 billion. He has been named as the richest person in Asia with a net worth of $88 billion and the 10th richest person in the world.

Early years

Mukesh was born on April 19, 1957 to Dhirubhai and Kokilaben Ambani in Yemen.

He has three other siblings, younger brother Anil, and two sisters, Nina and Dipti. Mukesh studied Chemical Engineering at the Institute of Chemical Technology, in Mumbai. He subsequently pursued an MBA from Stanford University, US, dropping out in 1980 to help build Reliance. Dhirubhai felt that entrepreneurship would be a much better teacher than classroom learning and enlisted Mukesh's help in scaling a yarn manufacturing project at Reliance. Since then, Mukesh has charted out an ambitious growth journey for Reliance, achieving one milestone after another.

Growth

Mukesh is credited with a period of intense growth in Reliance. He is responsible for creating several world-class manufacturing facilities which resulted in capacity expansion from less than a million tonnes to about 21 million tonnes per year.

He also pioneered Reliance's development of infrastructure and retail projects, championed the cause of digital by launching Jio, Reliance' digital services initiative. He led the launch of the most expansive 4G broadband wireless network offering end-to-end solutions.

Mukesh strategically invested and created Reliance's future by investing in retail and digital, two sectors which are cited to be the growth industries for the future. As part of this strategy, strategic disinvestments and acquisitions were made.

He focussed on de-leveraging, asset monetisation and creating a strategic direction for various business units. He also announced plans to sell the stakes in RIL's technology venture as well as its oil-to-chemical business to achieve an ambitious plan of becoming net debt-free by March 2021.The net debt free status was achieved well ahead of its deadline due to the stake sale in Jio Platform, netting an investment of INR 1.18 lakh crore.

On the retail front, Reliance's acquisition of the full spectrum of warehousing, retail, wholesale and supply chain operations from Future Group for INR 24,000 crore led to tremendous capacity expansion – their footprint grew to include 1800 stores of Central, Foodhall, Big Bazaar, EasyDay and Fashion BigBazaar. This has increased Reliance's revenues from its retail business, standing at 1.65 lakh crore, increasing RIL's overall retail revenue to 2 lakh crore, making it one of the largest retail operations in India.

Their partnership with Facebook was again a well thought out strategic enabler. As per data, 59% of retail is contributed by grocery and 41% is non-grocery segment. Through JioMart, they enabled access to countless kirana stores across the country, further increasing their retail footprint. Last year, Reliance Retail had around Rs 35,000 crore of revenue arising from groceries and Future Group grocery revenue was around Rs 16,000 crore. This would mean Reliance's grocery revenue alone was Rs 50,000 crore. Even at a 15% growth rate, they will be at Rs 65,000 crore revenue just from groceries, enabling them to a market leader in the retail and grocery segment.

Jio's rapid expansion in the retail segment raised concerns for e-commerce retailers such as Amazon, Flipkart as it is anticipated that JioMart's e-commerce market share in India will grow from around 1% now to 10 per cent in 2025. Knowing Reliance's aggressive growth strategies, it will not be long before Reliance makes master strides in the overall digital commerce ecosystem.

Reliance has also fortified its retail presence by the launch of private label brands to tap the grocery market valued at $608 billion, which is anticipated to grow more than 20% by 2024 as per research conducted by Forrester. The launch of private label brands, along with its massive retail and online strength is certainly giving established FMCG companies such as Nestle, Unilever and Coca-Cola concerns. Reliance is also aggressively offering high profit margin to retailers, as high as 20% as opposed to 10-12% offered on similar products by MNC FMCG companies.

Thus with one swift stroke, Reliance has managed market entry in retail, leveraged digital, and given much established brands right from Amazon, Flipkart, Nestle, Unilever a reason to watch out for Reliance in this category.

The second strategy for the future is digital – In this arena, The Reliance Digital stores contribute about INR 45,000 crore in revenue, which is one quarter of the total company's revenue. Three fourths of the total stores that Reliance has of the 10,000-odd stores are Reliance Digital stores.

The other businesses, notably, the fashion and lifestyle business contributes only INR 13,000-14,000 crore in revenue. As per equity research reports, Jio has 8 focus areas right now—agriculture, education, healthcare, gaming, media and entertainment, ecommerce and retail, e-payments and broadband. Across these eight verticals, there exists scope for both transaction-based and subscription-based revenue, giving Reliance ample opportunity to become a price leader.

Jio's biggest advantage is its access to customers through the mobility platform, which became the market entry strategy for many of Reliance's other businesses. Jio has around 40 crore customers on its mobility platform. Given the boost on digital, is is anticipated that the fibre-to-enterprise and fibre-to-home platforms would generate a higher revenue than their mobility platform. The Average Revenue Per User (ARPU) for mobility is around INR 140, fibre-to-home is round INR Rs 500-600 ARPU and much higher, closer to INR 1000, for the fibre-to-enterprise vertical.

It is anticipated that in 2021-22, the profit from Jio Platform would exceed the profit from the core business such as refining and petrochemical polymer business, truly making Reliance a global digital company.

Innovation

Mukesh realized the power of a digital ecosystem and led the creation of a platform for integrating all the high growth areas through digital.

After an evaluation of other big conglomerates such as Alibaba and Tencent which built massive enterprises at relatively lower debt and have a large aggregated consumer base led Mukesh to restructure Reliance in a way to pare its debt. Jio has now raised $10-plus billion from marquee investors such as Vista Equity Partners, KKR, Facebook, Silver Lake, and General Atlantic.

In April 2020, Facebook acquired a 9.99% stake in Jio Platforms, a wholly-owned subsidiary of Reliance Industries Limited, for an investment of $5.7 billion (INR 43,574 crore), making Facebook its largest minority shareholder. This was the largest FDI for minority investment in India till then. The deal with Jio enabled integration of WhatsApp with JioMart enabling people to have a seamless shopping experiences.

Facebook has openly stated its next growth target: to acquire its next billion users. Initiatives like internet.org and Facebook

Aquila were launched to provide internet access to remote areas10. Both initiatives did not succeed the way they were anticipated.

India has a large underserved population in context of internet access and this partnership is trying to address the untapped market. The Jio Mart platform seeks to serve millions of small shopkeepers in India. With WhatsApp Pay integration, the Jio and WhatsApp partnership aims to close the retail value chain. Jiomart is also trying to compete with Amazon and Flipkart.

As part of its future ready growth strategy, Mukesh has also charted out his vision for decarbonization of energy to create value-added products with almost no carbon emissions.

Crisis Management

Dhirubhai passed away in 2002. Mukesh and Anil jointly managed the company after his death. However, due to disagreements and difference of opinion, the brothers underwent a division of assets and business. Kokilaben split Reliance's assets via a noncompetition agreement under which Mukesh was provided the oil, gas, and petrochemicals businesses. Anil gained control of Reliance's finance, power and the existing telecom business.

It would appear that Mukesh retained only the traditional businesses and Anil got share of some of the more contemporary business. But Mukesh was not discouraged.

The launch of Jio gave Mukesh the ultimate platform for realizing his dreams in digital and telecom. While he had worked in setting up Reliance's previous telecom venture, Anil gained the control of the venture post the bifurcation of assets. However, RCom was struggling and eventually had to exit the telecom business in 2017. In 2010, Mukesh secured a spectrum license and the rest, as they is history.

Entrepreneurs can surely learn from Mukesh how to manage and circumvent challenges and come back stronger from crises.

Summary

Mukesh is credited with turning Reliance from an oil & petrochemical company to a digital, future-ready company. His bold ambitious vision and strategy for relentless growth has firmly put Reliance on the map. Entrepreneurs can learn a lot from a bold, ambitious global leader like Mukesh Ambani.

18.
Walt Disney

There are probably very few people who are not aware of Mickey Mouse Or Marvel; Or Disneyworld Or the man behind it all, Walt Disney.

Disney was born at the turn of the century, and is generally hailed as a modern day Leonardo da Vinci, such is his contribution to the arts. He is recognized as a pioneer in the American media and entertainment industry, given that the Walt Disney company's operations now span television, broadcasting, streaming media, theme park resorts, consumer products, publishing, across companies such as ABC, Marvel, Pixar, ESPN, building one of America's first, modern multimedia corporation.

A legend in the American animation industry, Disney holds the distinguished record for most Academy Awards received, at an impressive 32 Oscars apart from Golden Globe and Emmy and several other felicitations.

Disney was closely associated with the rise of the motion pictures as a medium. He was born in Chicago, Illinois, on December 5, 1901 to Elias and Flora Call Disney4. Subsequently raised at a farm in Missouri, Walt was interested in drawing from an early age. He began his career in Kansas, as an advertising cartoonist, gradually creating his first original animated cartoons in 1920.

The world famous cartoon character, which has received love and adulation, Mickey Mouse, debuting on the screen in Steamboat Willie, the world's first fully synchronized sound cartoon on November 18, 1928.

Disneyland, one of the first theme parks of its kind, was launched in 1955, as a place where adults and children could experience the wonder of childhood.

Created in 1962, Disney University (DU) was started as a global training program for employees of Disneyland, to acquaint them with the culture, heritage, values and policies of Disneyland, helping create wonderful experiences for guests.

Management Lessons Learnt from Walt Disney

Innovation

Disney's vision and foresightedness is legendary. He quickly adapted his core passion and reworked it for modern day technology, from drawing, to animation to Technicolor. Whether it was a new camera technique or new customer experiences at Disneyland, or adoption of synchronized sound, Disney was the pioneer of innovation, creation and adoption.

Vision

The first full-length animated musical feature film, Snow White and the Seven Dwarfs, premiered on December 21 in Los Angeles. Produced at a staggering cost [$1.5 million], the movie went on to set a precedent for animated movies for years to come, enthralling viewers who regard it as a watershed moment in the motion picture industry. Snow White was followed by other full-length animated classics as Pinocchio, Fantasia, Dumbo and Bambi. Disney had the vision to know and adapt to changing market technologies and deliver superior customer experiences.

Understanding the Customer

Disney was obsessed with understanding the customer. While building Disneyland, he famously got down on his knees, to experience the park from the viewpoint of its young visitors. He encouraged staff to mingle with the visitors at the park, remarking that it would help them understand the customer better, and it did.

Customer Experience

Walt was undoubtedly one of the world's best storytellers, and an undisputed showman. But his greatest talent was delivering great customer experiences. The Disney University is an example of his focus on customer experience.

Disney university was reinvented to provide and acquaint employees with Disney's culture, heritage, values and policies. Employees are acquainted with Disney traditions and philosophies. This helps the company create and provide the same superior level of customer experience across the globe.

Mental strength

Walt endured a tough childhood, delivering papers at the age of nine for his father's newspaper business. He woke up at 3:30 AM along with his brother, delivering newspapers before attending school and other chores. Alongside his work, he attended courses at the Kansas City Art Institute over the weekend and also took a correspondence course in cartooning. His tough childhood only provided him mental strength for hardships and business failures in his life later on.

Persistence

Disney wanted to move beyond formulaic short cartoon features. He commenced his mega project, "Snow White and the Seven Dwarfs," a project that took four years for completion. People within the industry came to know about Disney's ambitious mega project and dubbed it as "Disney's Folly," predicting its failure before the project even took off. Halfway through the production, Disney had to mortgage his house to help finance the film's production, which eventually ran up a total cost of $1.5 million, a huge sum for a production in 1937. Snow White eventually opened to rave reviews, earning an Oscar nomination, and winning Disney an honorary Oscar for the movie.

During all the trials and tribulations of producing a massive, large scale move, Disney persisted with single minded focus, not losing sight of the goal once, not letting his detractors get the better of him.

Handling Failures

Disney was no stranger to failures. Right from 1921, with the launch of his first company, Laugh-O-Gram Studio, to production over-runs with his later films, Disney saw multiple failures throughout his life. In 1923, Laugh-O-Gram went bankrupt and Disney had to restart his career all over again. Throughout his life, he came across obstacles, whether it was planning for the first Disneyland or mainstreaming some new innovation, Disney overcame it all with his persistence and focus. Entrepreneurs should learn the art of recouping failures and rising again to the challenge from Disney.

Summary

Disney embodied passion, innovation, learning and courage, creating wonderful customer experiences and a mega monolith media empire. His legacy continues, providing entrepreneurs many qualities to emulate and leaving them with the path to continue forward with innovation.

❑

19.
Phil Knight

'Just Do It' is not just an advertising slogan.

It's an expression against entropy of any kind.

It symbolizes energy, action and achievement.

Every aspiring sportsman has heard of the brand Nike. Every fitness enthusiast has come across the brand.

So what makes Nike synonymous with sports?

How did a shoe company completely capture popular imagination of people across the world?

This story began in 1938, when Nike's founder, Philip Hampson Knight was born.

Born in Portland, Oregon, to Bill Knight, a lawyer turned newspaper publisher, and his wife, Lota Cloy, Phil completed his education from the University of Oregon and the Stanford Graduate School of Business.

His interest in sports shoes was evident enough even at that age, as for his small business class, Knight authored a paper, *Can Japanese Sports Shoes Do to German Sports Shoes What Japanese Cameras Did to German Cameras?*

He was fascinated with Japanese high quality goods and wondered what would be impact of Japanese shoes in the American market3. Since he ran track, he gradually developed an interest in importing high-quality and low-cost running shoes from Japan into the American market. After graduating with a master's degree in business administration from Stanford in 1962, Knight set out on a trip around the world, during which he visited Kobe, Japan, in November 1962.

It was on his visit to Kobe where he discovered a superior brand of running shoes, Tiger, manufactured the Onitsuka Co. The high quality manufacturing, at such a low cost, impressed him and he sought a meeting with Onitsuka, who agreed5. That meeting led to Knight securing the distribution rights for Tiger in the western United States.

However, after that initial euphoria, there was a long waiting period. The first Tiger shoes took nearly a year to be shipped to Knight. In that period, Knight started working as an accountant in Portland. Ecstatic on receiving the shoe samples, he mailed two pairs to Bill Bowerman at the University of Oregon [Nike's co-founder], who was his track coach. Knight was hoping to secure a sale and an endorsement from an expert.

To Knight's surprise, Bowerman not only placed an order for the Tiger shoes, but also offered to get into a partnership with Knight, contributing product design ideas. On January 25, 1964, Blue Ribbon Sports (BRS) was launched, the company that would later become Nike. Both Bowerman and Knight invested $500 into the business, spending all that on their first order, which at $3.33 a pair, amounted to 300 pairs of shoes.

The first shipment landed in April of that year, and courtesy Bill's connections, it was fully sold out by July. Bill was one of the most recognizable coaches in America at the time, having trained multiple Olympic athletes. In their first year, BRS sold $8,000 worth of shoes; Knight then started scouting more employees for expansion. Bill was involved in product innovation, and had made multiple improvements to every new shipment from Onitsuka, by using more lightweight materials, and at that time he was almost co-designing Onitsuka's shoes for the American market.

Bill's innovation efforts paid off; one of Bill's designs, the Cortez, catapulted BRS into the mainstream and became one of the best-selling shoes in 1968. The 1968 Olympics, held in Mexico, were also a factor in the rising sales. In 1969, BRS sold $300,000 worth of shoes.

On seeing that rapid uptake of the product, Phil and Bill decided to evolve from just being a simple distributor organization. Their contract with Onitsuka ended in 1972, just before the Olympics in Munich, giving them plenty of time to prepare.

Around this time, two of the most iconic changes to the brand happened, made by people other than the founders.

In of the most fundamental changes to the brand, Jeff Johnson, Nike's first employee, suggested renaming the firm "Nike. Nike is the name of the Greek Goddess of victory, and would add a strong symbolism to the brand's image. Subsequently, Blue Ribbon Sports was renamed Nike in 1971.

The famous swoosh logo that is so synonymous with the brand, is the brainchild of the graphic design artist Carolyn Davidson, who was commissioned for the project for USD 35 in 1971. In September 1983, Davidson was allotted an undisclosed amount of Nike stock for her contribution to the company's brand.

The brand continued to rise and it became the largest sportswear company in America in 1989 on the back of brilliant marketing campaign "Just Do It". Also critical to the brand's success, were its endorsements from influential athletes across the sporting world who continued to wear it at global sporting events. From John McEnroe to Michael Jordan, the continuous patronage by sporting icons helped catapult Nike into sporting glory.

Diversification, Challenges and Pivot

Nike had travelled a long road. In their first year of business, they made an admirable $8000 profit. In 1965 their revenue had increased to $20,000 and they opened their very own store in Santa Monica.

Revenues climbed to $49 million in 1982 from just $60,000 ten years earlier and then to $9 billion by the mid-1990s. By 1998, 40% of the athletic footwear market was controlled by Nike.

However, the company faced a major challenge in the 1980s.

For quite some time, Nike struggled with connecting with its core target audience. By the mid-1980s, the financials of the company represented on the balance sheet the troubles of the brand in the market. Nike had been profitable throughout the 1970s. In fiscal year 1985, the company failed to achieve its target for two quarters (was in the red for two quarters) In fiscal year 1987, sales dropped by $200 million and profits declined.

These were due to a series of mis-steps, namely, the aerobics market and the casual shoe market.

Around this time, the fitness category market dynamics changed. A new category developed, aerobics, and Reebok emerged as a dominant market force, a category which Nike completely missed.

Starting from scratch in the early 1980's, Reebok was a $1.79 billion-a-year business in 1989, compared with Nike's sales of

$1.2 billion. In athletic footwear alone, Reebok had 26.7 percent of the market and Nike 23.3 percent.

The product development team developed an aerobics shoe, functionally superior to the existing Reebok product, but the styling was off the mark, and ended up being rejected by customers11. By the time Nike went back to the drawing board and came up with a revised product, Reebok had already established their brand, gained sales momentum, and established huge brand credibility in this market.

A similar catastrophe happened when Nike approached the casual shoe segment in early 1980s. Nike noticed that the running shoe business, which comprised of about one-third of their entire revenues at the time, was slowing down. Nike attempted a foray into casual shoes, but the results were not to the customers liking. Once again, it was a product failure.

Here was a classic case study. A brand which symbolized excellence in track and field was looking to reassess its identity. Missteps like the aerobics shoes and the casual shoes cost them dearly. Their target market got confused, retailers were not clear about the positioning anymore and became unenthusiastic, athletes started exploring other brands, and sales stagnated.

Nike found some redemption in the Air Jordan basketball shoe. By this time, the company had realized that segmentation and sub-segmentation was essential to driving sales and profitability.

They realized that they had to produce a great product, which would redeem their former reputation in running shoes. They focused their attention on basketball as a category, which fit in nicely within their core positioning.

The final outcome – a colourful basketball shoe – was banned by the NBA, resulting in great publicity for the brand.

The Rest is History

The brand has come a long way since, with global revenues amounting to $37.4 billion in 2020.

Controversies

Nike has faced continual criticism for their manufacturing practices. Initially, all their shoes were produced in the US, and were subsequently outsourced to factories in China.

Since the 1970s, Nike has been accused of using unfair practices to produce footwear and apparel. It has received backlash for its poor manufacturing practices and low wage per hour policies. Nike has strongly denied the claims in the past, suggesting the company has little control over sub-contracted factories. Beginning in 2002, Nike began auditing its factories for occupational health and safety.

Management Lessons Learnt from Phil Knight

Phil's story is hugely inspiring and has lots of learning for managers and entrepreneurs alike. His narrative is not just a story of triumphs and deals measured in net sales, profitability and return on investment (RoI). Rather, it is an extremely intriguing and emotional journey of a young entrepreneur. His fearlessness, enterprising skills, and never-say-die attitude have inspired countless entrepreneurs everywhere.

Vision

Phil had vision – of embracing high quality Japanese footwear as a clear differentiator in a market flooded with sub-quality footwear. His big vision was clear in his paper submitted in his business administration class and even in his trip to Japan. All of his actions were aligned with his overall vision.

Passion

Already a track athlete, Phil combined his passion with his vision. His understanding of the athletics market, sports as a category all helped him to provide the right insights for his business. His passion became the driving force behind his vision.

Having the Right Team

Phil's partnership with Bill was one of the biggest reasons for the success of Nike. Having the right functional expert within the team can be a huge enabler for an enterprise's success. Bill's expertise, his credibility and his passion for sports helped catapult Nike to even greater heights.

Belief

Early in his career, before founding Nike, Phil took a job selling encyclopaedias door-to-door, and another selling securities. He wasn't successful at either. He figured he just wasn't that good at sales. But when he started selling running shoes, he was very successful. It's our belief in our product that makes us a good salesperson.

Failures are okay

Nike had multiple missteps and stumbles, but it course corrected every time. Whether it was the casual shoes opportunity or the aerobics opportunity, every time, the team went back to the drawing board, asked themselves what would align with Nike's core values and delivered on the brand promise.

Summary

Ranked by Forbes as the 26th richest person in the world, Knight has an estimated net worth of US$ 39.2 billion (as of July 23, 2020). The brand that he helped developed with Bill has now expanded into a mega behemoth, with 2020 revenues cited at nearly $37.4 billion. He helped create an enduring image of sports, that of performance, excellence and craftsmanship, inspiring millions of sportspeople and entrepreneurs everywhere.

❑

20. Ted Turner

Ted Turner is the consummate media executive, leading a massive empire of broadcast media, turning a tiny billboard advertising company into a megalith media network.

Turner is credited with a lot of firsts, the first global TV news network, CNN, single theme channels showing only cartoons or movies and the 24 hours programming content.

Turner is an exceptionally important landmark in the media landscape. But Turner's legacy will not just be in media or broadcasting. His lasting legacy will be his philanthropic work and his contribution to the UN, for which he has set a personal example to founders and entrepreneurs everywhere.

Early Years

Turner was born in Cincinnati, Ohio. Ted's father, Ed Turner, purchased a small billboard company, naming it Turner Advertising in Savannah, Georgia. The business prospered initially, and Ted learnt the ropes of running an outdoor advertising company. In the subsequent years, the company was in huge debt in its efforts to buy out a competitor. Ed's health failed, and he took his own life. At the age of 24, Ted was saddled with the responsibilities of navigating a debt-ridden company.

Due to Ted's vision and hard work, Turner Advertising had transformed into the largest billboard company in the Southeast. At the same time, Ted noticed that his customers were increasing their spends on radio and television, prompting him to expand Turner's advertising's presence in broadcasting.

Ted's ambitious plans were for a market which at that time was dominated by three major networks, with each network having it own local affiliate in the major regional markets. The question of having a fourth or fifth station was nearly outlandish.

Cable television was still a nascent market with only few operators servicing remote areas. Thus Turner began a phase of expansion, investing in a number of radio stations, and also a UHF station in Atlanta. Around the same time, he renamed Turner Advertising to Turner Communications Group and the station was named WTCG.

Subsequently, he acquired another station in North Carolina, and purchased the broadcast rights to TV shows and movies. After suffering initial losses, the fortunes of Turner Communication Group turned. Turner's business strategy was also supported by changing FCC regulations which permitted cable television services to transmit programming from remote stations1. He knew that consumers would demand more content and continuously kept on increasing the company's content through technology, satellite communication and content.

In the next few years, Turner bought the Atlanta Braves baseball team, and a controlling interest in the Atlanta Hawks basketball team and began broadcasting its games live, increasing the content available for broadcasting line-up.

The combination of sitcoms relevant to a rural audience, live sports, old movies and professional wrestling helped expand the audience base of Turner Media.

In 1980, Turner made yet another ambitious bet. He sold the TV station that he had acquired in Charlotte and launched a 24x7 news channel. Broadcast professionals wrote off his investment and strategy as laughable.

Channels ran local news for a limited duration in the evening, with the understanding that it was the news anyone needed. Stubbornly, Turner continued with his plans for *Cable News Network (CNN)* and added a second channel, *CNN* Headline News, in 1982.

CNN generated a profit by 1985 and Turner added *CNN* Radio and *CNN* International to the portfolio1. *CNN* revamped news presentation completely. Aware of the emergence of live reporting, *CNN* crews were equipped with portable satellite transmission equipment, enabling them to report live from anywhere in the world.

· Ever alert to new developments in broadcasting technology, he equipped CNN crews with portable satellite transmission equipment, so they could report on breaking news, live from anywhere in the world.

Management Lessons Learned from Ted Turner

Risk taker

Turner has always been a bold and prolific decision maker. He purchased MGM in 1986, but decided to sell it soon after, only retaining the film library.

This seemed to be a foolhardy business decision at that time, costing around $100 million, but Turner's astute business acumen proved otherwise. Within one year, the film library generated returns of $125 million.

Around this time, the home viewing market emerged and expanded, and the demand for videotape films increased. MGM's library included not just classic MGM movies, but also the catalogue from United Artists, Warner Brothers and RKO, included timeless classics. In the early 90s, Turner Media acquired Hanna-Barbera, the animation studio, and launched the Cartoon Network, the much loved, 24x7 cartoon channel. Subsequently, Turner added Castle Rock Entertainment and New Line Cinema to the broadcasting portfolio and in 1994, founded Turner Classic Movies, to showcase old timeless movies.

With each and every decision, Turner was going against popular business advice and trends. But he had tremendous conviction in himself and faith that he could decipher the future business and media trends correctly. Entrepreneurs need to imbibe this trait from Turner, having the ability to make decisions quickly and with limited information, and take calculated risks is a skill that any business owner needs to master.

Resilience

Turner was faced with adversities early on in life. His father, Ed committed suicide, leaving young Ted to manage a debt-ridden company. He knew that he had to turn around the company and had very limited resources to do so.

Ted did not give up, he was resolute and determined that he would turn around the business and he did. At every stage in his life, the odds were stacked against him, but Turner pursued and expanded his business rapidly.

Philanthropy

Ted is known for his $1 billion gift to support the United Nations, and for the creation of the United Nations Foundation, a public charity which broadens U.S. support for the UN.

He also established the Turner Foundation which works in the area of improving air and water quality, sustainable energy, protecting the environment, safeguarding wildlife habitat, and advocating programs for population control.

He also established The Turner Endangered Species Fund 1997, which works in the area of biodiversity conservation. He co-founded the Nuclear Threat Initiative in 2001, which works in the area of preventing nuclear proliferation.

Summary

Ted Turner will continue to inspire people to believe in their dreams, and strive to achieve it, even when no one thinks its possible. His legacy through his philanthropy work has impacted millions of people and shall continue to do so.